NEEDLE LACE & NEEDLEWEAVING

For Jo,
I enjoyed having
you in my class!
Jill Nordfors, 1976.

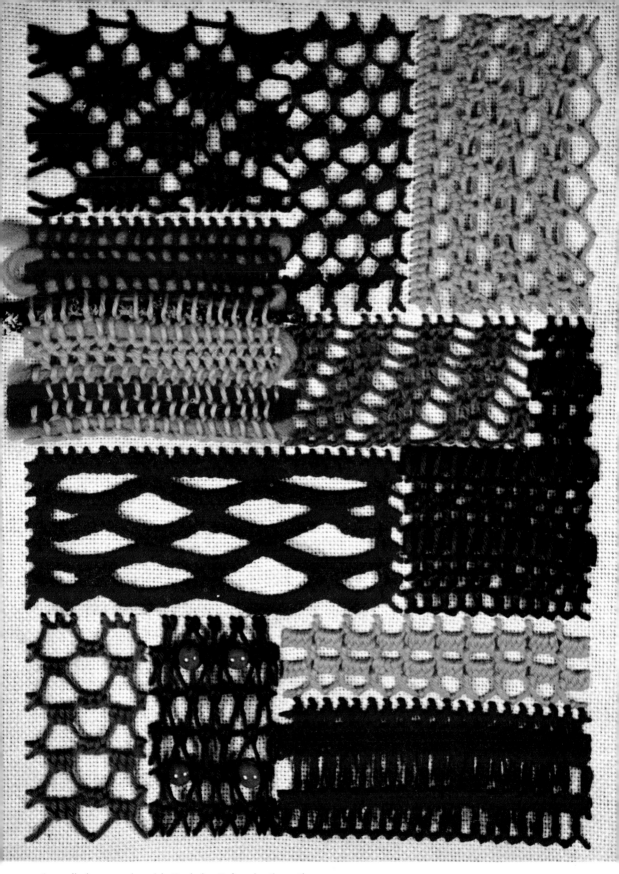

A needle-lace sampler of buttonhole stitches, by the author.

NEEDLE LACE
&
NEEDLEWEAVING
A new look at
Traditional Stitches

Jill Denny Nordfors

Photographs by Beverly Rush
Line Drawings by the Author

VNR VAN NOSTRAND REINHOLD COMPANY
NEW YORK CINCINNATI TORONTO LONDON MELBOURNE

For my three loves: Spence, Chris, and Erica

Van Nostrand Reinhold Company Regional Offices:
New York   Cincinnati   Chicago   Millbrae   Dallas

Van Nostrand Reinhold Company International Offices:
London   Toronto   Melbourne

Published by Van Nostrand Reinhold Company
A Division of Litton Educational Publishing, Inc.
450 West 33rd Street, New York, N.Y. 10001

16 15 14 13 12 11 10 9 8 7 6 5 4 3 2

The author and Van Nostrand Reinhold Company
have taken all possible care to trace the ownership
of every work of art reproduced in this book and to
make full acknowledgment for its use. If any errors
have accidentally occurred, they will be corrected in
subsequent editions, provided notification is sent to
the publisher.

Library of Congress Cataloging in Publication Data

Nordfors, Jill Denny.
  Needle lace and needleweaving.

  Bibliography: p.
  1. Needlepoint lace. 2. Drawn-work. I. Title.
TT800.N67   746.2′2   73–10893
ISBN 0–442–26059–8

Acknowledgments

My deepest thanks to the many people who have helped
me complete this book, a project I could not have done
alone.

First, to my husband, Spence, and my two children,
Christopher and Erica for their patience and understanding.

To Jacqueline Enthoven, for inspiring me to begin this
venture, and for naming me heir to her wealth of knowledge on the subject of traditional needle lace.

To Bev Rush for being a friend and a great photographer.

To Virginia Isham Harvey, Preparator, for sharing the Costume and Textile Study Collection at the University of
Washington.

To Flo Wilson and Jean Wilson for sharing their ideas and
their shoulders.

To all the artists and fellow stitchery enthusiasts for lend-
ing me their work to use for illustrations.

To Pat Lantz for typing endlessly, and to Ellen Fay for
typing my final manuscript.

To Ellen Lowrie, Geri Douglas, Sandy Owens, and their
helpers for assuming my role as mother of a pre-schooler.

To my very capable editors, Nancy Newman and Judith
Vanderwall.

And finally, to my parents, Mr. and Mrs. Tom Denny of
Victoria, British Columbia, Canada, for their great en-
thusiasm and for instilling a deep pride in accomplishment.

All photographs by Beverly Rush, unless otherwise indicated

Designed by Elaine M. Gongora

Contents

Foreword

There is a quality about Jill Nordfors' work, something exciting and deeply satisfying, which made me urge her to share her talent with everyone.

Her book takes the subjects of *Needle Lace and Needleweaving* a step further because of its detailed description of how to master the technique. It will be an invaluable aid to those who want to use these stitches in a contemporary way, making discoveries of their own. At first glance, the stitches may look difficult. Actually many of them are so easy that children master them with ease, and delight in the results.

Jill Nordfors is particularly well qualified to write on this subject. She is a gifted artist who has demonstrated her ability to develop original uses of traditional stitches. The beauty and clarity of her diagrams will delight the reader, as will Beverly Rush's superb photographs.

I am very much looking forward to seeing the work which will be done under the influence of Jill Nordfors.

Jacqueline Enthoven

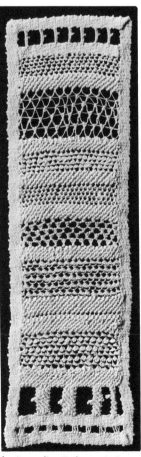

Samplers of needle-lace stitches made for Jacqueline Enthoven in France by Marguerite Berlier Oviste, who was decorated by the French Government for excellence of her work as a needle-lace artist. Courtesy of Jacqueline Enthoven.

Teneriffe - lace tablecloth. Courtesy of Mrs. Earl M. Chalk. The motifs used throughout the book, on opening pages of sections, are from this tablecloth.

How to Begin

WHAT IS NEEDLE LACE?

Needle lace is composed of an almost infinite variety of lace-like embroidery stitches made with a needle and useful for filling any shaped space. They may be worked on a background fabric or airily suspended on an open warp. They are attached only at the perimeter of the design, thus forming an open net similar to knitting or crochet. The difference between needle lace and the more familiar surface embroidery is that needle lace is *not* attached to the background at every stitch.

Traditional needle-lace stitches have been folded up in the bottom drawer since our great-grandmother's day. Now it is time to give them an airing, to delve into the past, and to use our heritage as an inspiration for contemporary embroidery.

WHAT IS NEEDLEWEAVING?

Needleweaving is a form of embroidery where a warp, a series of long threads, is stitched into a background or wrapped around a supporting frame. The filling is woven into the warp with a tapestry needle, using simple over-and-under darning and needle-lace stitches, either separately or together. It is similar in construction to some forms of the traditional drawn-thread work.

Needle lace and needleweaving work so well together that they belong in one book; one that is an invitation to students, teachers, housewives, children, hobbyists, and professional artists to try this exciting traditional art form that has such great possibilities for contemporary creations.

I have not tried to present a historical documentary of traditional needle-made laces, but instead have researched and compiled a great variety of the stitches derived from these laces. The stitch names may be unfamiliar, and perhaps you will know them by a different name. In each case they are identified by description or by the name that occurred the most frequently in reference material.

Whatever the name, it is my sincere hope that creative embroiderers everywhere will use this book as a basic reference for detached stitches. Try them first in the traditional way, then let your imagination and ideas be the guide.

Together, let us begin now to learn all about detached needle-made stitches and share the joy in rediscovering a part of our heritage.

Basic Materials

If you have already tried embroidery, sewing, needlepoint, macramé, or weaving, chances are you will have most of the necessary materials for needle lace and detached stitches right in your home. A quick checklist of basic materials follows, and each item on it will be discussed in depth below.

1. Tapestry needles of different sizes for both fine and heavy threads—they are the ones with large eyes and blunt ends—and small sharp-pointed needles for very delicate threads.

2. Some yarn, not too heavy, not too thin, with a good twist and a smooth surface—fuzzy yarn will hide the stitches.

3. A piece of monkscloth, cotton homespun, or similar loosely woven fabric, preferably with an even weave (ie., equal numbers of even threads going in both directions). Also, any other background materials you may wish to experiment with, such as needlepoint canvas.

4. A large embroidery hoop or frame to stretch the fabric. For small samples use a small hoop.

5. Fine sharp-pointed scissors.

6. Straight pins.

7. A collection of found objects such as beads, shells, moss, sticks, or rocks to incorporate in the stitchery.

NEEDLES AND THREADS

Traditional needle-made laces were worked on a delicate scale, with very fine white or off-white linen thread, using small sharp-pointed needles.

Needle-lace stitches, being detached from the fabric background, are worked in rows, each row forming a base for the next. In larger-scale work, to keep from splitting the thread, the stitches are best made with a tapestry or blunt-ended needle, rather than one with a point. Tapestry needles come in various sizes (1¾ to 2¾ inches long), rounded at one end and with large eyes to accommodate any weight thread. They can often be purchased in knitting shops where they are sold for piecing sweaters together.

If a loosely woven background fabric is used as a base for the stitches, a tapestry needle will easily go through it. It is a good idea though, to keep sharp-pointed needles handy for those times when you may want to use a more closely woven background or work in very fine thread. For working on warp threads stretched on a frame,

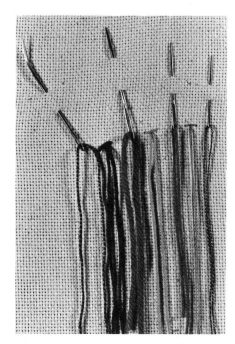

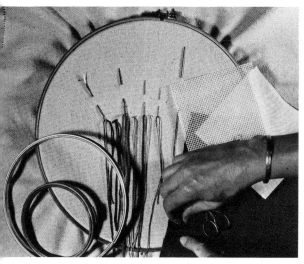

Figure 1-1. Basic materials for needle lace and needleweaving: loosely woven fabrics, needlepoint canvas, embroidery hoops, curved needle, tapestry needles, weaving needle, scissors, and pins.

Figure 1-2. A curved needle and three sizes of tapestry needles threaded with suitable yarns for needle lace and needleweaving. *Left to right:* D.M.C. Perle Cotton size 3, cotton macramé cord, four-ply knitting worsted, Lily Double-Quick Crochet Cotton, D.M.C. Retors à Broder Cotton, J.P. Coats Crochet Cotton, and D.M.C. Perle Cotton size 5. Most of the stitch samples in this book are done in these materials, because they show the stitches clearly, but finer or heavier yarns can also be used.

Figure 1-3. Needlepoint canvas with eight to ten holes to the inch is an excellent background for learning the stitches.

Figure 1-4. A sample of single buttonhole filling in two colors of knitting worsted on a background of needlepoint canvas.

try a curved needle or, for large areas, a 6-inch, metal, blunt-ended weaving needle.

To see each step clearly as you learn the stitches, it is best to use a yarn or thread with a smooth surface, a good twist, and a color in bold contrast to the background fabric. At first you may prefer to work on a large scale, perhaps using knitting worsted on needlepoint canvas (10 holes to the inch), or basket-weave (two-over-two) monkscloth. Shiny D.M.C. Perle Cotton, size 3 or 5, or matte D.M.C. Retors à Broder Cotton are slightly finer. Some sizes of crochet cotton are even finer, and all come in a wide color range and make good samples.

Once the stitches become more familiar to you experiment with more highly textured yarns, with macramé cords, or with fishing line. See what each will do. Work on a very large scale with heavy cords or on a very delicate scale with fine sewing thread. Build a collection of yarns. Buy several ounces of each color, as detached stitches are "thread eaters". It is very disappointing to be working with a special thread, only to run out three quarters of the way through.

BACKGROUND FABRICS

There are as many choices of suitable background fabrics for needle lace as there are stitches. An off-white, basket-weave monkscloth or a Hardanger cloth with two threads crossing over and under in both directions or needlepoint canvas (10 or 12 holes to the inch) are all excellent for learning the stitches. The threads are evenly spaced and easily counted.

As you work each row, the stitches will form a net-like structure over the background, either lacy and very open where the fabric shows through, or tight and closed, completely covering the fabric. If the background shows, then its color, texture, and compatability with the stitching thread becomes a consideration.

Perhaps the lace is to be made in the traditional way, where the finished piece is removed from the background. In this case, tack down, or couch, the outlining threads through a strong transparent tracing paper on which the design has been drawn with indelible ink, and through two layers of oilcloth, heavy brown paper, or linen beneath the drawing. You are couching through all three layers at once. When the lace is complete, snip the couching stitches between the two bottom layers.

11

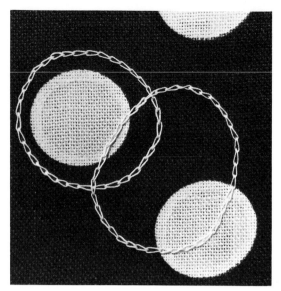

Figure 1-5. A printed fabric background for needle lace with circular pattern repeated in a chain-stitch outline of heavy sewing thread.

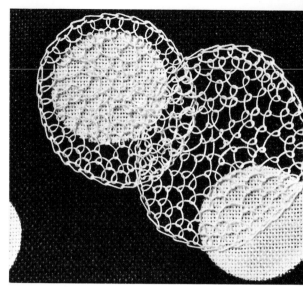

Figure 1-6. The outlines are filled in with open, lacy, or single buttonhole filling.

As the rhythm of working the stitches becomes more familiar to you, experiment with many different background fabrics. What about trying a printed fabric rather than a solid color (fig. 1-5)? Use the pattern of the print as a basis for your own design, varying its size and shape, stitching either on the background or over the print itself. Vary the weight, color, and texture of threads to see what happens.

Preparing the Background for Stitching

STRETCHING THE FABRIC ON A HOOP OR FRAME

As needle-lace stitches are attached to the background fabric only around the perimeter of the design area, the fabric behind them must be held taut. The simplest way of stretching the material is to use an embroidery hoop. They come in many sizes and in both metal and wood. They may be found in hobby and yarn shops everywhere. I enjoy the little 4-inch ones for delicate work as much as the 12-inch ones for larger-scale work. Children are fascinated with embroidery hoops. Often they will put their own fabric in and begin to stitch, much as they would pick up a piece of paper and begin to draw.

If you do not have access to a hoop, a piece of fabric may be stretched over a simple wooden frame or canvas stretchers, both available in art-supply stores. Figure 1-7 shows how to stretch the fabric. Lay the fabric right-side-down on the table or floor, then lay the frame right-side-down on top of the fabric. Trim away the fabric so it extends about 2 inches (less for smaller scale frames) beyond the frame on each side (1). Using a staple gun or thumb tacks, fold each corner in toward the frame at right angles, and tack down (2: A, B, C and D). Trim off the points of these corners after they are fastened to make them less bulky.

Fold in edge E, and put a tack in the center (3). Do the same for edge F, then G, then H. Put more tacks in each edge, working from the center toward the corners and stretching opposite edges against each other as you go. When finished, you have a nice tight surface to stitch on.

A heavily sized needlepoint canvas need not be stretched, but may be thumbtacked to a wooden frame for easier handling.

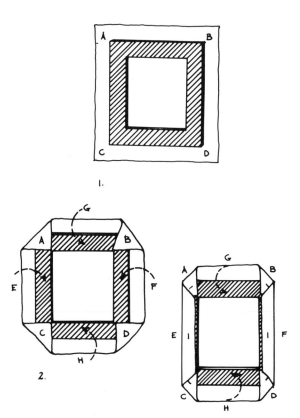

Figure 1-7. Stretching a fabric on a wooden frame or oil canvas stretchers.

Figure 1-8. A good way of keeping the work taut, while working detached stitches, is to pin the edges to a foam-rubber slab with T-pins.

OUTLINING THE STITCHING AREA

If the background fabric is loosely woven and of a large-scale even weave, quite often the first and last rows of needle lace, and the beginning and end of each row, may be worked into the fabric itself. An outline of basting thread as a guide or, in the case of needlepoint canvas, a chalk or pencil line may be all you need.

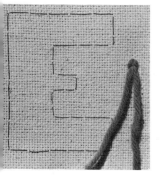

Figure 1-9. Sewing thread basting (running stitches) as outline on basket-weave (two-over-two) monkscloth.

Figure 1-10. Closely worked knotted buttonhole filling completes the *E*.

Figure 1-11. Renaissance-lace handkerchief border. An outline of tape or braid is filled with tiny needle-lace stitches. Courtesy of Mrs. Charles Ogden.

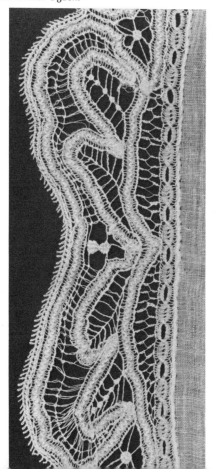

Braid Outlining

In traditional needle-made laces, such as the Renaissance lace in Figure 1-12, the design area was first outlined with braid or tape. The braids, either handmade or machine-made bobbin lace of varying designs, were basted first to a stiff, tracing-paper backing, imprinted with a pattern, through two layers of oil cloth, brown paper, or linen cloth. Needle-lace stitches were then worked in the open spaces between, hooking into the edges of the braid where necessary. When all the spaces were filled and the lace completed, the basting threads between the two bottom layers were cut, and the piece fell free from the backing. Our present-day stitchery could borrow this technique. There are many manufactured braids, trims, cords, and ribbons in the fabric shops, which, when combined with needle-lace stitches, could produce spectacular stitcheries.

Figure 1-12. Fragment of Renaissance lace. Braid or tape outlines leaf-shaped areas, which are filled in with needle-lace stitches. Courtesy of The Costume and Textile Study Collection, School of Home Economics, University of Washington.

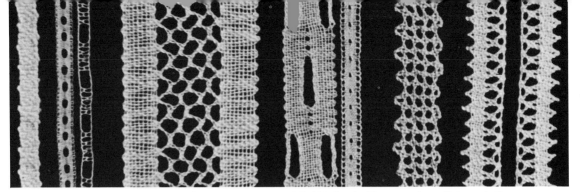

Figure 1-13. A collection of handmade and machine-made bobbin-lace braids or tapes for outlining, as in Figures 1-11 and 1-12. Courtesy of Jacqueline Enthoven.

Stitches for Outlining

To anchor the lace stitches firmly to a stretched background fabric, any shape may be first outlined in chain stitch, backstitch, or any other outlining stitch you may want to try. To work the backstitch, knot the end of the working thread and bring the needle to the surface at A (fig. 1-14,1). Go down into the background at B, coming up again at C (1). For the second stitch, go down in the same hole as A, coming up at D (2). Continue working the backstitches from right to left, each the same length, until the area to be stitched is outlined. To turn a corner on a square or rectangle, follow Diagram 3.

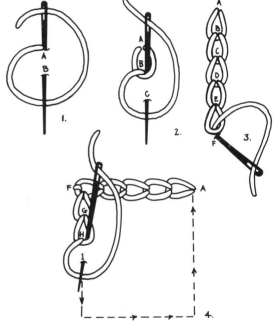

Figure 1-15. Outlining the design area with chain stitch.

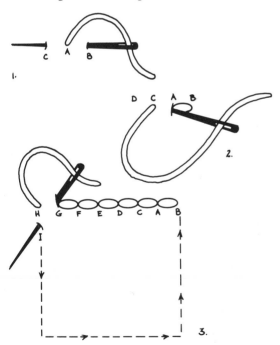

Figure 1-14. Outlining the design area with backstitch.

The choice of outlining stitches depends on the effect you want. Backstitch is smooth, straight, and linear; chain stitch is bumpy, curved, and more decorative. Try the chain stitch on a scrap of fabric. Knot the end of the thread, then come up from the back of the work at A (fig. 1-15,1). Make a loop, counterclockwise, with the working thread. Go down into the fabric where you came up, at A, coming out again below A at B. Pull through and down over the loop to make the first chain. For the second chain (2), again make a counter-clockwise loop with the working thread. Go back down in the same hole as B, coming up at C. Pull through over the loop to make a second stitch. Work each succeeding chain this same way, following a circle, a wavy line, or a straight line. When you run out of thread or reach a corner, tack down the last loop with a small stitch (3:F). Begin the outline again, in any direction, by working over the loop of the last chain stitch (4:G).

Couching is the term used for tacking any object or thread to the background fabric with a second thread. This method is particularly handy if the thread to be tacked down is too bulky to be pulled through the fabric. An easy way to begin a design in stitchery is to dangle a thread onto a background, letting it fall where it may. Rearrange the curves in the most pleasing pattern, pin, couch in place, then fill the outlined open spaces with embroidery stitches. Needle-made laces of the past used an outline of couched threads as an anchor for the detached filling stitches at both ends of each row. You may want to plan the enclosed area carefully, using a geometric shape (fig. 1-16,1), or arrange the couching stitches in a pattern first, before sliding the needle with a second thread between these stitches and the background (2). If the couching stitches are to be cut away to let the finished piece fall free from the backing, work them in a contrasting color. This makes them easier to see, and lessens the chance of cutting into the piece itself.

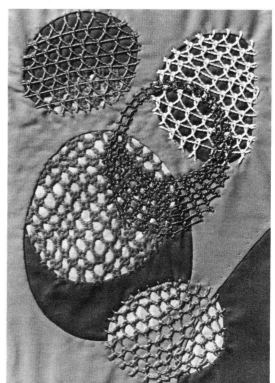

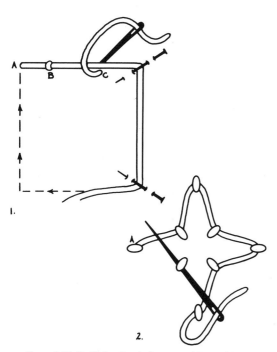

Figure 1-16. Outlining the design area with couching.

Cut-Through Appliqué

Cut-through appliqué is a technique used extensively in the San Blas Islands of Panama and recently popularized in the United States by stitchery artist Jean Ray Laury. The simple curves of the cut-out shapes make an ideal background for needle-lace stitches (figs. 1-17 a,b).

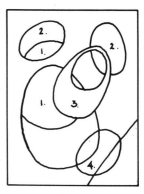

Figure 1-17a, b. Cut-through appliqué with needle-lace stitches: (1) double buttonhole filling, (2) detached buttonhole filling with straight-stitch return (or couching with buttonhole stitch), (3) raised chain band used as filling, (4) knotted buttonhole filling.

Try a small sample first. Baste together a stack of three to five layers of fine cotton—sheath lining, percale, or broadcloth—in compatible solid colors. Cut out a series of circles, beginning with the largest one on the top layer, exposing a new color for each layer as the circles get smaller. Leave the bottom layer intact. Thread a slender, sharp-pointed needle with matching sewing thread.

Begin the appliqué at the top layer by rolling the raw edge under ⅛ to ¼ inch with the needle. Hold the folded edge in place with the left thumb

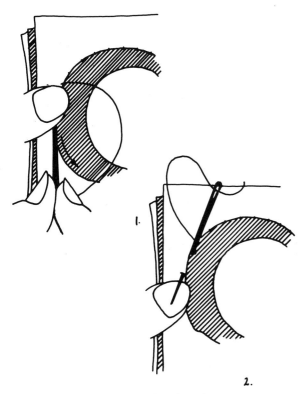

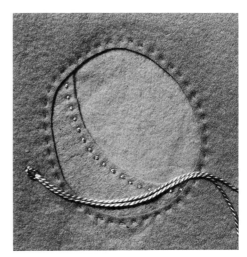

Figure 1-19. Cut-through appliqué in felt. Edges are sewn with running stitch in sewing thread and D.M.C. Perle Cotton size 3.

Figure 1-18. Cut-through appliqué.

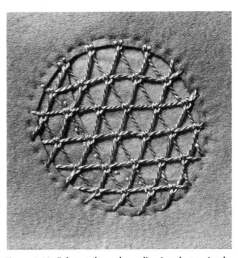

Figure 1-20. Felt cut-through appliqué makes a circular outline for a net of double buttonhole filling with straight-stitch return.

(fig. 1-18,1). Knot the end of the sewing thread, then come up from the back, through all layers of fabric, barely catching the folded edge. Make a blind stitch by going down to the back of the work to the right of the fold and then coming up just below, again catching the fold. Or, secure the fabric with a row of running stitches close to the folded edge. Repeat the appliqué for each layer. A quick way to achieve the cut-through look with very little work is to use felt. Figures 1-19 and 1-20 show three layers, in contrasting colors, held together with running stitch and embroidered in D.M.C. Perle Cotton.

To work detached stitches in the cut-out area, attach the first and last rows, as well as the beginning and end of each row, to the turned-under edge. Finish off threads at the back of the work by stitching into the bottom layer of fabric.

DRAWING OUT THREADS

Author and historian Irene Emery, in her book, *The Primary Structures of Fabrics,* describes cutwork or drawn-thread work by writing,

"...first, parts of the ground fabric are cut away or withdrawn; and second, stitches are used both to prevent fraying of cut edges and to embellish the whole by reworking bared elements or refilling cut-out spaces."

In Italy, in the early sixteenth century, the lace Reticello (meaning "square holes") evolved from drawn-thread work. Groups of threads crossing each other were pulled out, leaving "square holes". These holes were then reinforced at the edges and filled in with areas of closely worked buttonhole stitches and woven or corded bars. Later in the sixteenth century the cloth was discarded, and the lace became Punto in Aria, worked entirely on a goundwork of thread.

For present-day embroidery, the technique of drawing or pulling threads out of a fabric to form

17

Figure 1-21. Square of Italian Reticello lace, a traditional method of drawn-thread work. Courtesy of The Costume and Textile Study Collection, School of Home Economics, University of Washington.

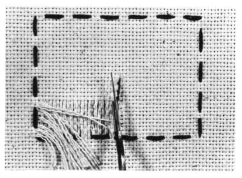

Figure 1-22. Drawn-thread work. After outlining the design area with contrasting thread, cut the filling threads to be pulled out.

Figure 1-23. Drawn-thread work. In pulling out the filling threads, bind the raw edges left by the cut threads with buttonhole stitch (top) or by weaving the loose threads into the wrong side of the fabric (bottom).

a background for stitching has great potential. There are several ways of approaching drawn-thread work. Either the warp or the filling (weft) threads or both may be pulled out. Try horizontal open stripes, made by removing several groups of filling threads from selvage to selvage. Or, outline an area with basting and then cut the filling threads only, down the center (fig. 1-22). Pull the cut threads out to both sides toward the basted line, then weave them back into the fabric (fig. 1-23). If you prefer, cut the filling threads at both sides of the basted area and remove them completely. Bind the raw edges with buttonhole stitch (fig. 1-23). For a border effect or plaid effect, pull out threads in both directions (fig. 1-24).

Pulled-work is like drawn-work, but no threads are removed. Instead, the warp or filling of a loosely woven fabric is pulled apart or distorted with the tip of the needle, exposing the threads woven in the opposite direction.

Once you have chosen the technique and worked out a pleasing arrangement of open and closed spaces, go ahead to develop the embroidery or needleweaving over the exposed threads. Figure 1-25 shows buttonholed bars in a simple repeat pattern (see fig. 2-122).

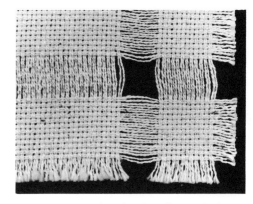

Figure 1-24. Drawn-thread work. Pulling out both warp and filling threads to make a border or create a plaid effect.

Right: *A geometric pattern of surface stitches, by the author, on a zig-zag printed fabric. Areas of raised chain band build up a third layer of texture.* Below left: *Painting by Christopher Nordfors at age 5.* Below, right: *Sampler of needle-lace stitches, by the author, using the painting by Christopher as a basic outline and color key.*

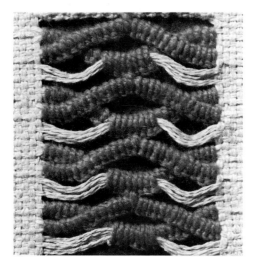

Figure 1-25. Drawn-thread work. Warp threads left in the fabric are covered with close-worked buttonholed bars.

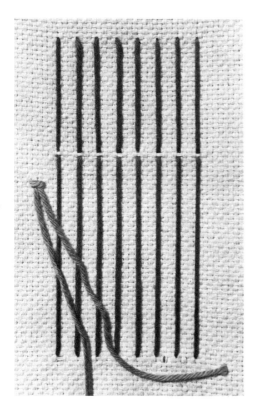

Figure 1-26. Laid threads, stitched evenly on a monkscloth background, in D.M.C. Retors à Broder Cotton, form a base for needle-lace stitches.

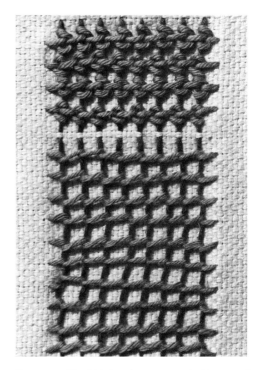

Figure 1-27. The laid threads are covered with rows of raised chain band (top) and stemstitch band (bottom).

MAKING A BASE OF LAID THREADS ON THE FABRIC

Many detached stitches are made in two stages. First, a base of straight stitches is laid on, or at-tached, to the background fabric. Second, another series of stitches is looped or knotted over this base. The layers of fabric, stitches, then more stitches make a rich, deep, three-dimensional texture.

The base stitches may be long or short, evenly or unevenly spaced, separate or overlapping, and shaped in a curve, a circle, or a rectangle. The top stitches may be worked in the same yarn as the base, or contrasted with bulkier or finer yarn in a second color. For more texture, work the stitches close together in a heavy yarn; for less texture, far apart in a fine yarn.

The next section of the book describes each stitch along with its appropriate base. Here, let us try a few ideas for the base itself.

For evenly spaced, parallel-laid threads, knot the end of the thread and come up at A (fig. 1-28). Go down into the background at B, then up again at C. Make another long stitch to D. Continue this pattern, following the direction of the arrows, from E to F, G to H, and then from I down to J, where the thread may be finished off at the back of the work.

For a random base of crisscross threads, perhaps to be used for the raised-stem spiderweb stitch (see fig. 2-67), bring the thread up at A (fig. 1-28, 2). Then work freely, making a long straight stitch to B, then from C to D, E to F, G to H, to I and down to the back of the work at J. A random

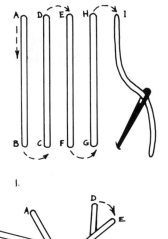

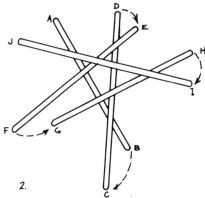

2.

Figure 1-28. Making a base of (1) parallel or (2) random laid threads.

base works very well on a fabric background in a 4- to 6-inch embroidery hoop, each base stitch stretching from one edge of the circle to the other.

Often a version of herringbone stitch, which makes a pattern of crossing diagonal lines, is used as a base for detached stitches (see the section on borders and interlacing stitches beginning on page 89.)

STRETCHING A WARP

Warp threads are like laid threads in that they can be layered on a fabric background or suspended freely in an open space. The warp is held under tension by being stitched into a stretched fabric or supported by any rigid object. Wire, cardboard, pins, plastic, or wood can all be used.

Stretching a Warp on a Frame

Start with a simple wood frame. Canvas stretchers, usually available at hobby and frame shops, are inexpensive and come in sections to any size. Variety stores have an assortment of ready-made frames, usually sold for small items like diplomas and 8 x 10 family photographs, but equally suitable for stitchery.

For the warp, use a linen rug warp from a weaving supplier or heavy cotton macramé cord from a hobby or yarn shop.

There are several methods of stretching the warp (fig. 1-29). If the wood is sturdy and not likely to split, drill evenly spaced holes in the frame from front to back (1) or from outside to inside (3). Knot the end of the cord. Then using a tapestry needle, if necessary, thread the cord through the drilled holes. Before securing the loose end, pull either upward or downward on each of the threads from A to make the warp taut.

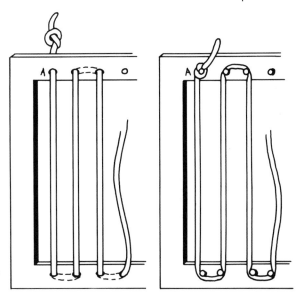

1. 2.

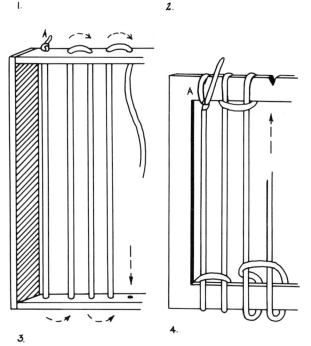

3. 4.

Figure 1-29. Stretching warp on a frame.

Figure 1-30. Random warp threads stretched on a small square frame as a base for needleweaving, by Jo Reimer.

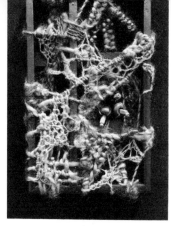

Figure 1-31. Warp threads freely wrapped around an abacus, as a base for needle-lace stitches, by Maggie Turner.

Secure with a knot at the opposite end. Alternately, the warp can wrap around evenly spaced brads or small nails (2) or around the frame itself (4). To hold the cords in place, make notches along the outside edge of the frame with a triangular-shaped file.

A small rectangular frame or an embroidery hoop, freely wrapped with a random yarn warp, can make an exciting base for needleweaving (fig. 1-30). More warp threads may be added as the filling stitches progress.

Stretching a Warp between Fabric Edges

Try embroidering in a "hole". Cut two pieces of fabric of equal size and place on a flat surface, right sides together. Draw a circle on the fabric, using a plate or lid as a guide if you don't have a compass (fig. 1-32, 1a). Cut out the circle, through both layers, leaving a ½- to ⅝- inch seam allowance, and then machine stitch around the marked line A. Trim away excess fabric by cutting notches in the seam allowance. Pull the back layer through the hole to the front (2). Press around the hole, and thumb tack the outside fabric edges to a frame. Work warp threads back and forth across the circle's edge. Hide the knots of new threads between the two layers of fabric.

Artist Virginia Thorne makes "holes" to stitch in by mounting fabric on a stiff cardboard mat (fig. 1-32, 3 and 4). Decide on the finished size of the circle, then cut it out of cardboard. Lay the cardboard flat on the wrong side of the fabric. Cut out the fabric inside the circle, leaving 1 inch showing, then cut out triangular notches with their points almost touching the cardboard rim. Trim away the outside fabric edges to about 1½ inches (3). Using a white glue, such as Elmer's, fasten the circle's edge to the back of the cardboard. Then fasten the outside edge. Fold in corners A, B, C, and D (4), and then the opposite edges F and E, G, and H (4). Allow the glue to dry, and begin stitching the warp threads.

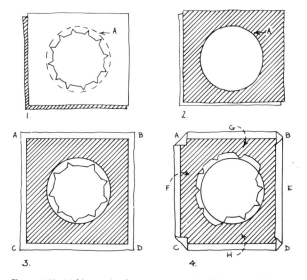

Figure 1-32. Making a circular cut-out area in fabric (1 and 2), and mounting fabric on a circular cardboard mat (3 and 4), as a base for detached stitches.

Figure 1-33. *Moonbeams*, by Virginia S. Thorne. Needle-lace stitches on a random warp, stretched across a 6-inch circular area, bordered by fabric.

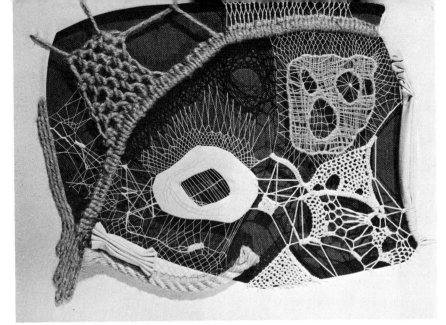

Figure 1-34. *Web in Canvas I*, by Evelyn Svec Ward. Random warp threads, held at the edges with heavy canvas, support needle-lace stitches in a range of materials from heavy sisal to light-weight cotton. Courtesy of Mrs. Sanford B. Ketchum; photograph by William E. Ward.

Dividing a Warp with Coral Knots

Once your warp is ready, you can outline any shape with coral knots (fig. 1-35), and fill the space with needle-lace stitches. Practice first on a scrap of fabric. Bring the needle and knotted thread up at A (1). Arrange the working thread in a counter-clockwise loop, holding it in place with the left thumb. Insert the needle diagonally from right to left into the background fabric just above the working thread at B. Come out just below, at C. With the tip of the needle over the base of the loop, pull through and down to the left to make

the knot. Repeat this step from D to E (2). Now, work several long straight stitches on the background fabric from A to B (3). Choose a random beginning point to the right of the base threads at C. Work a coral knot over each base thread, sliding the needle from right to left behind the base thread rather than into the background.

Use this technique to outline any shape on a stretched warp—straight lines or curved (4)—as an anchor for the detached filling stitches. Incorporate any loose ends of thread in with the warp, hiding them in the work as the filling stitches progress.

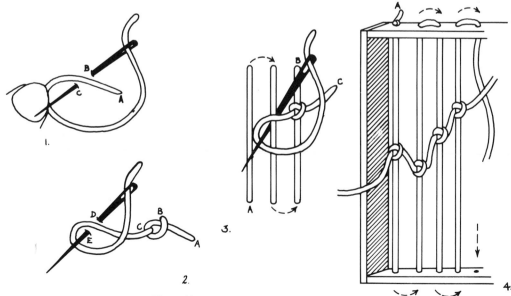

Figure 1-35. Dividing a warp with coral knots.

Collecting and Attaching Found Objects

Found objects are man-made things or natural materials you may find anywhere. They add special interest to a piece of embroidery. They might include rocks, shells, fur, bones, drinking straws, leather, ribbons, beads, sticks, cones, moss, dried flowers, feathers, seed pods, seaweed, buttons, glass, or any bits of nostalgia at hand.

Decorating embroidery with *shi sha* glass mirrors is a technique from India combining stemstitch, Cretan stitch, and chain stitch. Little nets or cups made of detached buttonhole or stemstitches are perfect for attaching rocks. String beads at random on a warp for needleweaving, attach some leather circles, weave a stick into a row of buttonhole stitches, or thread some yarn up through a barnacle shell.

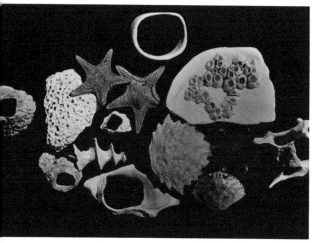

Figure 1-36. A collection of found objects from the beach: shells, coral, starfish, bones, barnacles, and crab backs. Courtesy of Margaret Denny.

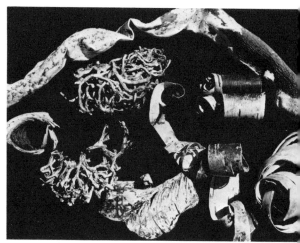

Figure 1-37. For interesting texture try seaweed, curled bark, and driftwood. Courtesy of Margaret Denny.

Figure 1-38. Jig-saw puzzle pieces of bark, from the trunk of an evergreen tree.

Figure 1-39. Nature's geometry can be incorporated in a stitchery or used as the basis of a design.

STEMSTITCH NET

Figure 1-40 illustrates the technique for attaching a shell to the background fabric with a stemstitch net or mesh. To practice this technique, use a shell, a large seed, a flat rock, or a piece of felt cut in any shape. Holding the shell in place with your left thumb, come up close to the edge at A (1) to begin a series of horizontal stitches. Take the

thread across to the right side and down at B (1), then up again at C, slightly below B. Cross back over to the left side and down into the fabric close to the edge at D (2), then up at E. Complete the horizontals with another stitch from E to F (2). Depending on the size and weight of the object you are attaching, work more or less horizontal stitches. A small rock the size of a penny may only need two threads across, a 4-inch circle of leather may need as many as eight. To hold the weight of a heavy object, the mesh should be tighter. Increase the number of horizontal and vertical stitches accordingly.

From F bring the thread up at the lower left edge at G (3). Climb the ladder of horizontals, working toward the top with a stemstitch over each one. Make a stemstitch by sliding the needle behind the horizontal from the upper right to the lower left. Pull through and down to finish the stitch. Use the left thumb to hold each stitch in place as you work the next. End the first vertical at the back of the work at H (3). Come up at I (4) to climb back down the ladder, this time sliding the needle behind the horizontals from the lower left to the upper right. Go down into the background at J (4). Finish the series of verticals from K to L (5), climbing the ladder again and working the stemstitches as for the first line, G to H. Finish off the end of thread on the wrong side of the work by taking a few small stitches into the fabric behind the shell.

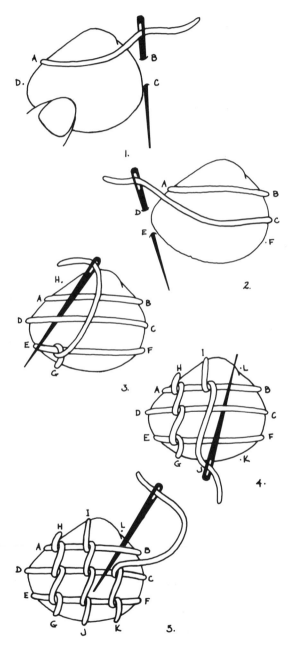

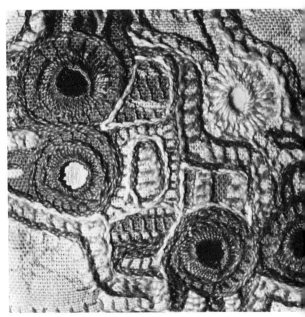

Figure 1-40. A net of stemstitch for attaching objects to a background fabric.

Figure 1-41. *Shi sha* glass technique used to attach large sequins to the surface of a pincushion, by Mary Ann Spawn.

SHI SHA GLASS

In India, small pieces of *shi sha* glass or mirrors are attached to garments and household embroidery of all kinds, using a very simple but beautiful combination of stitches. A net of stem-stitch (see fig. 1-40) makes the base, which is then completely covered with a layer of Cretan stitch (for Cretan open filling, see fig. 2-70). Sometimes it is combined with chain stitch (see fig. 1-15).

Try out the *shi sha* technique by attaching a small round piece of felt, a small flat rock, or a washer. Shiny large sequins are available in most department store notion counters and hobby stores. For practice, they make a good substitute for the real mirror glass, which is less readily available.

Try a sample following the diagrams in Figure 1-43. Take a small backstitch in the fabric to anchor the working thread (see fig. 1-57). Center the mirror over this backstitch, holding it in place with your left thumb. Come up at A (1) to begin the stitching. Lay a vertical thread over the mirror by taking a small horizontal stitch into the background fabric close to the lower edge from B to C (1). Return to the top edge with a second vertical

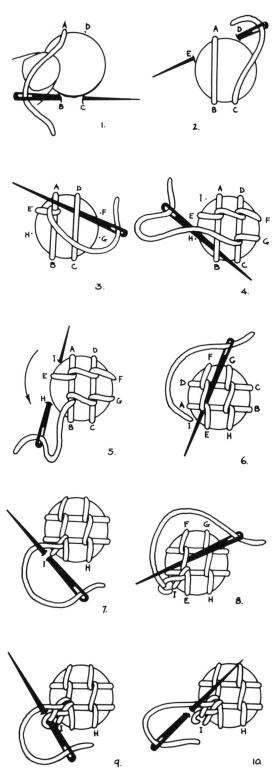

Figure 1-43. *Shi sha* glass technique for attaching objects to a background fabric.

Figure 1-42. A flat rock held on fabric surface by the *shi sha* technique, with outer circle of interlacing stitch on a base of double herringbone.

26

thread by going down into the background at D (2), then coming up at E (2), to begin the horizontal stitches.

The base threads, when finished, look like the familiar grid for a game of tic-tac-toe. Begin the horizontal part of the grid at E (3), working a stemstitch over the line A B (3). To make the stemstitch, slide the needle from the lower right to the upper left behind A B. Pull through and up to the left snugly, holding the loop in place with the left thumb while working the next stitch. Work a similar stitch over the line D C (3), going down into the background at F to end the first horizontal. For the second horizontal, come up at G (4), working the stemstitches this time from the upper left to the lower right, behind the line D C, then behind the line A B. Go down to the back of the work at H (4). If the thread is short, finish it off at this point by taking a few small stitches into the background fabric behind the mirror.

With a new length of thread, come up I (5), slightly away from the mirror's edge, to begin the Cretan. Turn the work so I is at the lower left, then work the first stitch by sliding the needle from above, behind the intersection of the line A B and the stemstitch E F. Pull through gently (6). The outside rim of the circle may be made in several ways. The diagram here shows a chain stitch (7), or a second Cretan (10). To make the chain, working in a clockwise direction, take a tiny stitch in the background, beginning in the same hole as I (7). With the working thread behind the tip of the needle, pull through to make a chain stitch. Go directly back to the center to work the second Cretan stitch over the line E F, right next to the first (8). For the second chain, go down into the fabric in the same hole as you came up, take a small stitch, and pull through over the working thread (9). Continue the Cretan on the inside, chain on the outside, in a clockwise direction, until the base threads are covered and the circle completed. Finish off the thread by taking a few small stitches behind the mirror in the back of the work.

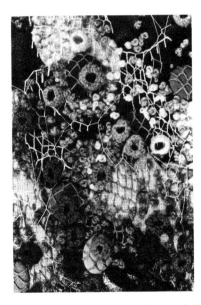

Figure 1-44. *Rocks and Barnacles*, by Karin Morris. Smooth flat beach rocks are attached to the fabric with nets of lacy buttonhole filling. "Barnacles" are detached buttonhole cups.

Figure 1-45. Round rocks, attached with *shi sha* nets and spiderweb stitches, combine with beads and French knots for a rich texture, by Susan Roach.

ATTACHING OBJECTS WITH BUTTON-HOLE STITCH

The versatile buttonhole stitch is ideal for making little nets or cups to hold objects to a background fabric. The stitches may be worked in rows either in one direction, back and forth, or around in a circle.

In Figure 1-45, nets made with open or lacy buttonhole stitches, worked from left to right, hold smooth oval rocks in place. To try the net (fig. 1-46), hold a rock, a piece of cardboard, or a piece of cut-out felt, on a background fabric with the left thumb. Knot the end of the thread and come up close to the upper left edge at A (1). Take a small vertical stitch into the background at B, pulling through gently, over the working thread, to make a loose buttonhole stitch. Go down into the fabric at the upper right edge at C (2), making a long diagonal stitch to the left edge, behind the rock, and up at D (2).

From D, work a buttonhole stitch from left to right, over each loop of the first row, and down at E (3). Work a third row from F to G (4). Continue increasing the number of stitches in each row as necessary to fit over the widest part of the object. (For a square, the rows will be equal length.) If the object is larger than 2 inches in diameter, save thread by working the buttonhole rows in both directions. Decrease the number of stitches in each row as you reach the lower edge (4:H to I). Anchor the last row by working a single buttonhole stitch into the background fabric (4:J to K). To finish off the thread, take a few stitches behind the attached object on the wrong side of the work.

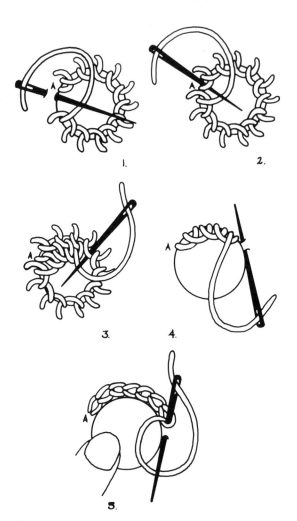

Figure 1-47. Buttonhole cups for holding objects to a background fabric.

Figure 1-48. Buttonhole cups form nests of detached buttonhole stitch for round white rocks, by Mary Ann Spawn.

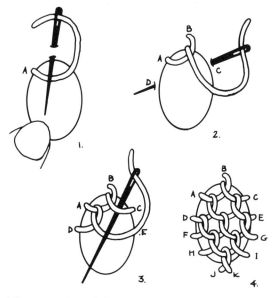

Figure 1-46. Buttonhole nets for attaching objects to a background fabric.

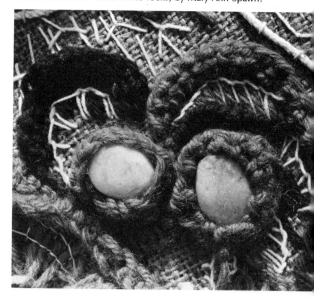

Figure 1-49. Chottie Alderson attaches jewels to needlepoint canvas with acorn cups of detached buttonhole stitch. Needlepoint stitches will eventually cover the exposed backing.

Figure 1-50. Long straight stitches laid on as a base for needleweaving also attach a clay piece to a background canvas, by Marge Krejcik.

Figure 1-51. Straight stitches form a random warp for needleweaving, raised at one end by sections of egg carton, by Inez Lucker.

A buttonhole cup (fig. 1-47), rather than forming a net over the attached object, holds it in place with a tight circle of closely worked detached buttonhole stitches (see fig. 2-4).

Hold the object on the fabric with the left thumb until there are enough stitches to secure it. Knot the end of the working thread and come up at A (1), close to the edge. Work buttonhole stitches at right angles to the object's edge in a clockwise direction back to A (1). Or, work a row of loose backstitches or chain stitches parallel to the object's edge, as an anchor for succeeding rows of buttonhole stitch (4 and 5). For the second row, work a buttonhole stitch in the loop between each stitch of the first row (2 and 3). The stitches will be close together. To keep them flat to the surface of the object, decrease stitches from time to time, by working into every alternate loop rather than every loop. Work more rows as necessary to hold the object firmly. To end or change a thread, weave back down through the rows to the fabric (the buttonhole stitches should be close enough together to permit this), and out to the back of the work. Take a few small stitches behind the attached object and clip off the thread.

ATTACHING OBJECTS WITH STRAIGHT STITCHES

A series of long straight stitches can attach a bead, barnacle shell, or even an egg carton to a fabric, and at the same time make a raised warp for needleweaving.

Tie a knot in the thread and come up at a random point A (fig. 1-52,1). Slide a good-sized bead, with a hole large enough to accommodate many threads, over the needle and down the thread to the fabric at A. Make a circle of warp threads by going down first at B (2). Come up at C, then back down through the hole in the bead, through the fabric, and across the back of the work to D (2). Work similar stitches from D to E, and from E to F, as close together or as far apart as you wish. When there are enough long threads to complete the circle, choose any pair or group to fill in with plain weaving or Cretan stitch (3). For a delightful tent or umbrella-like structure, try random needleweaving using several thread colors. Begin each thread on the perimeter at X (3), and end by going down through the hole in the bead to the back of the work. Cretan open filling can also be employed.

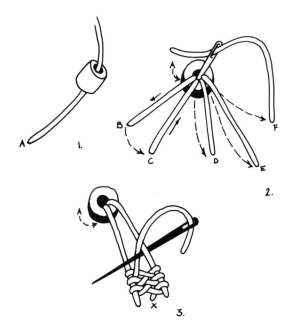

2.

Figure 1-52. Attaching objects with straight stitches to make a raised warp for needleweaving.

Figure 1-53. *Stone and Stitches*, by Karin Morris. Straight stitches suspend a white rock between shaped black leather strips.

Making a Sampler

Figure 1-54. Sampler, by Susan Roach, made during her first attempt at needle-lace stitches.

Figure 1-55. Another first-attempt sampler, by Maxine Freeland, in varied yarns and threads.

A sampler is a personal thing. It is your way of remembering each stitch, how it is made, what threads work best, and what variations you can invent. The sampler need not be a finished masterpiece suitable for framing and hanging on the wall, but it should be a bright, colorful source of information. You might prefer to work each stitch in all its varied forms on a separate notebook-sized piece of fabric. Keep each one as it is finished in a large loose-leaf binder. If you want the sampler to look more finished, practice first on another piece of fabric. Then, once the stitch becomes more familiar to you, work it on the sampler.

I remember my own first sampler of embroidery stitches so well. It was made on burlap in very bright knitting worsted yarns. It made kitchen chores in a rather drab little apartment much happier by smiling down at me from the wall over the sink. By studying the stitches as I worked, I could make up my mind by the time I was finished, just exactly what stitchery project to start on next.

The following paragraphs describe some tips, techniques, and ideas that may be helpful in the actual working of needle-lace and detached stitches.

WORKING WITH THREADS

Types of threads or yarn suitable for needle lace were discussed earlier in this chapter. Here, we are concerned with the technique of handling the thread, of beginning and of ending.

First, determine the length of thread you will need. You may have a few trial runs before you can decide on a suitable length, but here are some guidelines. You will need enough to finish one row, preferably two or three, depending on the length of the rows. The stitches are only attached to the background or the outline at the first and last row, and at the beginning and end of each row. Therefore, it is important to have enough thread to reach either end, rather than being caught in the middle with a loose end and nowhere to hide it. Too long a thread will tangle and knot, distorting the loose net of stitches as you try to pull it through.

Sometimes the thread will kink as you work. To straighten it out, hold the piece you are working

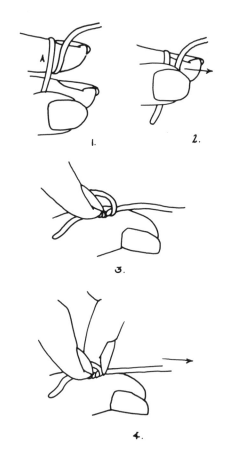

Figure 1-56. Tying a knot in the end of a thread.

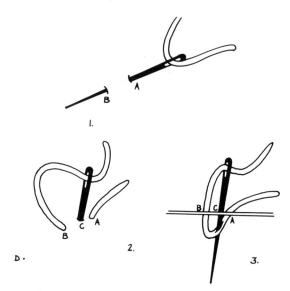

Figure 1-57. Securing the working thread with a backstitch in the fabric.

on up in the air, letting the needle and thread dangle freely. When it stops unwinding, resume the stitching.

If you are working the stitches on a background fabric, and the background is to remain as a permanent part of the work, start the stitching by coming up from the back of the work with a knot at the end of the thread. To make the knot, wrap the thread once around the left index finger (fig. 1-56,1). Place the thumb firmly on the point A where the two threads meet, rolling them together off the end of the index finger (2). Press the loop against the thumb with the index finger (3). Place the second finger at the top of the loop (4). Pull the long end of the thread gently, with the right hand, to make the knot.

If you dislike the lumpiness of a knot, secure the working thread with a backstitch in the fabric, which can be hidden under the stitching as you work (fig. 1-57). Take a small stitch on the right side of the fabric (1: A to B). Go back down at C (2) to make the backstitch, and in doing so, split the lower thread with the tip of the needle (3). Come up at any point to begin stitching, as in D

(2). Weave in or clip off the loose end at A when the work is completed.

If the finished lace is to be removed from the background, you will begin by couching threads to the fabric to make an outlined border (see fig. 1-16). Often, when the lace is complete, these couched threads will be bound with close buttonhole stitches as in a buttonholed bar (see fig. 2-122). Any loose ends of threads may be caught in and hidden by the buttonhole stitches. When the outlining is a heavy cord or braid, the beginning and end of the threads may be woven back into the border without showing.

Figure 1-58 shows how to make an inconspicuous little knot, handy for securing threads at the edges of the work. Split the outlining thread X Y (1) with the needle at A so the knot will stay in the correct position. Work a coral knot (see fig. 1-35), by arranging the working thread in a loop, coun-

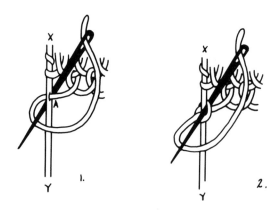

Figure 1-58. Knot for securing ends of thread at the edge of the work.

terclockwise, and then sliding the needle behind X Y at A and out over the working thread. Leave this first knot slack enough to thread the needle back through it from behind for a second knot (2). Pull the second knot very tight, and trim the end off flush. The larger the thread, the bigger the knot will be; therefore, this technique is more useful and less conspicuous for finer work.

If, for some reason, you do run out of thread halfway across a row, there are several alternatives for ending one thread and beginning a new one. If the stitches are very close together, making a solid area in the lace, weave the ends back into the work itself. If the net is very open and airy, two threads may be spliced together by whipping, a technique described on page 100. Use a fine sewing thread for the whipping, matching the color as closely as possible to the thread in the lace. Clip the loose ends close to the whipping and resume stitching.

Weavers use a small, tight, inconspicuous knot for joining filling threads or for repairing broken warp threads (fig. 1-59). This knot is also appropriate for lace making, as you can draw the knot very tight and clip the loose ends flush without worrying about the knot pulling out. It is equally suitable for working with needle lace and detached stitches. If you are careful to let the knots fall on the wrong side of the work, they will be covered up as the stitching progresses.

Leaving ends of approximately 1½ inch, cross thread A over thread B (1). Holding the threads in this position between the right forefinger and thumb, pick up the long end of thread B, looping it around counterclockwise and between the crossed short ends (2). Now, fold short end A toward you and tuck it under the thumb (3). Fold short end B away from you and hold it down between two fingers (4). Hold all the threads tightly while pulling the long end B (4) upward with the left hand to tighten the knot. Let go, then pull hard in opposite directions with both hands to tighten again. Clip off the ends flush with the knot, and resume stitching.

If the needle-lace stitches are being worked on a background, and the background is to remain a part of the finished net, it is possible to go down into the fabric in the middle of a row, finishing off the thread by taking a few small stitches in the back of the work. Knot the end of a new thread, and begin the stitching again by coming up in the same hole as you went down into.

WORKING WITH STITCHES

To make the rows of needle lace or detached stitches in a square or rectangular shape, every alternate row must have the same number of stitches, forming a layered brickwork pattern (fig. 1-60).

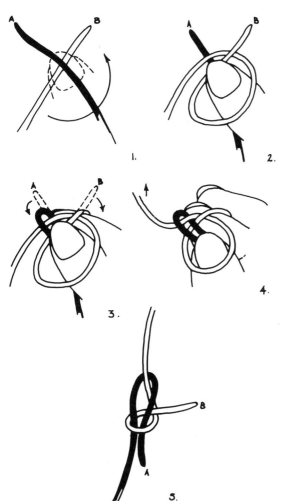

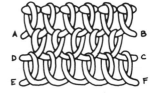

Figure 1-60. To fill a square or rectangular shape with needle lace, every alternate row must have the same number of stitches.

Figure 1-59. Knot for joining threads, called a weaver's knot.

It is important to keep an even tension as you work the necessary looped buttonhole stitches, as the development of the pattern depends on their uniformity. With practice you will see what each loop will do if worked loosely or pulled tight. The height of each row depends on the tightness of the stitches. A tight stitch may only be ⅛-inch high, where a loose loop could be ½-inch high. The spacing between rows, at the edge of the work, will be the same as the height of the stitches. If the lace stitches are worked on a loosely woven, even-weave background, such as basket-weave, two-over-two monkscloth, count threads between rows for even spacing.

In working large loops between stitches it may help to use a smooth flat stick or plastic ruler as a spacer (fig. 1-61). If the stitches are made too tight around the spacer, it is difficult to remove after the row is finished. An interesting design could be built up by leaving spacers in the lace. Use popsicle sticks, tooth picks, twigs, bulky yarn, ribbon, or leather strips as spacers.

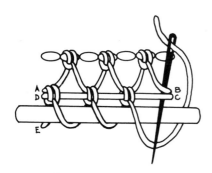

Figure 1-61. To make even loops between stitches, it may help to use a smooth flat stick as a spacer, or gauge.

Straight pins are also a great help in keeping an open mesh that has large loops between stitches flat against its background. Pin into the fabric, at right angles to the loop, as each one is finished. Sometimes the net will be very springy and awkward to handle as you build up the rows, looking more like a pot scrubber than a delicate needle-made lace. To straighten it out, pin each loop of the last row to the background, spray heavily with spray starch, leave several hours or overnight to dry thoroughly, remove the pins, and resume stitching.

You may wonder what to do with the working thread to get it from the end of one row to the beginning of the next. If the background fabric is to be a permanent part of the work, the working thread will either go down to the wrong side of the work, then back up, slightly below, to start a new row; or, if the design area is outlined with chain stitch (see fig. 1-15), or backstitch (see fig. 1-14), the working thread will hook into these stitches (fig. 1-62, 1). When the lace is made in the traditional way, to be removed from the background when finished, the outline will be couched threads (see fig. 1-16). At the end of a

row, wrap the working thread once or twice around these threads, then begin the next row (fig. 1-62, 2).

With the basic preparations made, let us go on to try the needle-lace stitches.

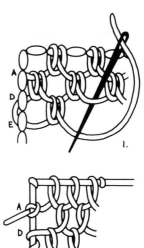

Figure 1-62. Ways of starting a new row with a continuous thread.

Needle Lace: The Stitches

Detached needle-lace stitches can be divided into two separate categories. The first are those constructed with a single thread in which rows of loops, worked back and forth, have formed their own net or mesh. The second are those constructed in two stages: one or two layers of straight stitches or drawn threads on the bottom, and another layer of looped, woven, or knotted stitches on the top.

The diagrams and photographs here show samples in which most of the stitches are stitched on a permanent fabric background. Traditional needle lace was worked on a backing, and then the backing was cut away when the lace was finished. Many of the following stitches may be treated either way, depending on the effect you are striving for. Preparing the background for both methods has been previously described.

Lacemakers usually worked in very fine linen thread, mostly white and ecru. Here the samples are made on basket-weave monkscloth and Hardanger cloth using D.M.C. Retors a Broder Cotton, and sometimes D.M.C. Perle Cotton size 3, both available in a wide range of colors. Using larger-scale thread and contrasting colors for each layer makes the construction of the stitch easier to see.

To learn the stitches, try several types of medium-weight yarn, and then go on to experiment with the full range, from bulky yarns to fine sewing threads.

Stitches On Their Own

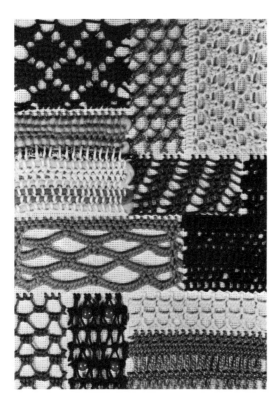

Figure 2-1. Sampler of buttonhole stitches, by the author, showing what a single looped stitch will do when it is worked separately, in groups, in various weights and textures of thread, close together, far apart, or in combination with other yarns, beads, sticks, and ribbon.

Figure 2-2. Needle lace made in France in 1945. The tape or braid outline is filled with many detached-buttonhole variations. Courtesy of Jacqueline Enthoven; photograph by Jacqueline Enthoven.

LOOPED-FILLING STITCHES

Detached buttonhole stitch and its multitude of variations could fill an entire chapter. The basic stitch is a simple loop. Once it becomes familiar, the gamut is yours, by working it close together or far apart, singly or in groups, in one direction or in both directions, in rows or in a circle. It may be knotted or plain, close and textured, or open and lacy.

The following diagrams will start you off with some ideas. From these go on to invent your own; the combinations are almost infinite.

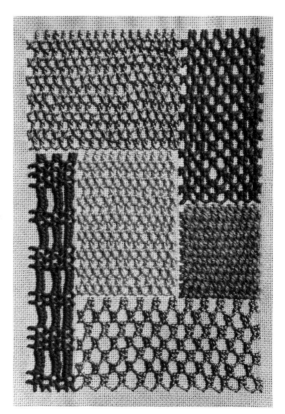

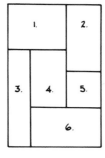

Figure 2-3. A patchwork of buttonhole stitches. (1) Single buttonhole filling, (2) double buttonhole filling, (3) spaced buttonhole stitches in groups of two and three. Return row alternating groups of one and two, with buttonholed bars. (4) Knotted buttonhole filling, (5) closely worked couching with buttonhole stitch, (6) knotted double buttonhole filling.

Detached Buttonhole Filling

The detached buttonhole filling is traditionally worked very close together in both directions, with no background fabric showing between stitches. The needle laces of the past made with this stitch were usually started on a base of two long straight stitches. However, for more contemporary and larger scale work, a base of outlining, chain, or backstitch holds the first row more securely and allows more flexibility in planning the design shape.

In Figure 2-4 (1) after completing the anchoring row of backstitches, knot the end of a new thread and begin the detached buttonhole stitch by bringing the needle up at A. (The space between A and the top of the backstitches determines the depth of the buttonhole row.) Slide the needle from above, under the first backstitch, being careful not to pick up any background fabric. With the working thread under the tip of the needle, pull gently to form a loose loop.

Work a similar loop in each backstitch until you reach the right-hand border (2). For an even row, it is important to keep each stitch the same as the last. It may help to use the left thumb to hold them in place as you go.

To end the first row, take the needle and thread to the back of the work at B, then up again at C (2).

The return row is worked between each of the stitches of the first row, while you still do not pick up any background fabric. Working from right to left this time, slide the needle from above, behind the first loop formed by the previous row. With the working thread looped under the tip of the needle, pull through gently (3). Work from right to left with a similar buttonhole stitch in each space. At the left-hand border, end the return row by taking the needle and thread to the back of the work at D (3). Come up at E, and repeat Rows 1 and 2, in sequence, until the rhythm of the stitch becomes familiar to you. To hold the last row in place either work each stitch into the background fabric (4), or tack each loop down with an extra stitch (5). To finish off and hide ends of threads in the back of the work, weave them into the wrong side of the outlining stitches. An anchoring stitch taken in the back of the fabric itself may show through in the front.

With a good basic knowledge of detached buttonhole filling, go on to experiment with the following variations.

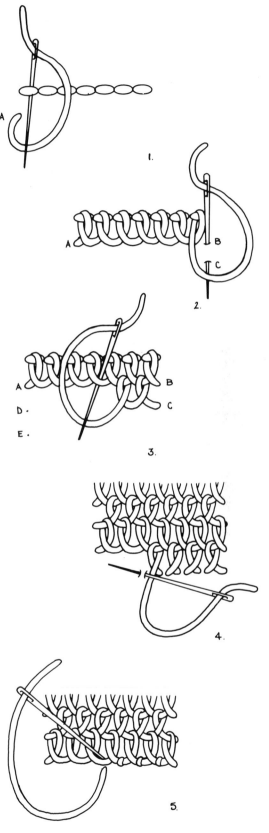

Figure 2-4. Detached buttonhole filling.

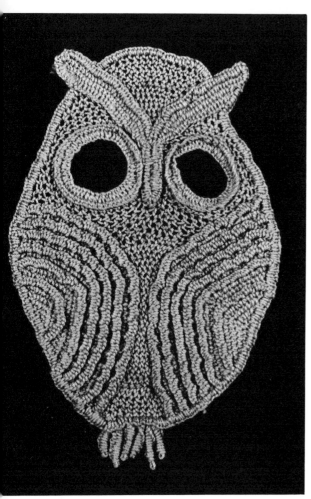

Figure 2-5. Owl, in closely worked detached buttonhole filling, by Nancy K. Evans.

Figure 2-6. Detached buttonhole flower by beginning stitchery student Nancy Fitzgerald. A triangular shape is made by working rows of detached buttonhole filling back and forth, decreasing one stitch on each row.

Open, Lacy, or Single Buttonhole Filling

Detached buttonhole filling, when worked loosely with the stitches farther apart, becomes open, or lacy, buttonhole filling. It may be used evenly to fill a regular shape, or most unevenly to fill an abstract shape.

For a change of pace, try working a circle of lacy buttonhole in an outline of chain stitch. Place any large coin, jar lid, or cup flat on the fabric, and trace around it with tailor's chalk or colored pencil, preferably the color of the yarn to be used. You might want to make several circles, perhaps overlapping. Stitch over the chalk line with chain stitch.

With a long thread on the needle, tie a knot at the end and come up under a chain stitch on the circle's edge, at A (fig. 2-7, 1). Working clockwise toward the center, make a loose buttonhole stitch over the inner side of each chain. Turn the work and hold the loops in place with your left thumb as you go.

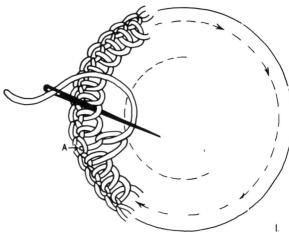

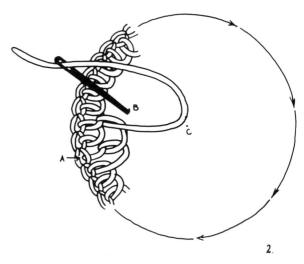

Figure 2-7. Open, lacy, or single buttonhole filling.

Figure 2-8. Circle of open, lacy, or single buttonhole filling.

Figure 2-9. Needle-lace butterfly. Wings are outlined with cord, then filled with delicate buttonhole-stitch variations. Courtesy of The Costume and Textile Study Collection, School of Home Economics, University of Washington.

When the first round is complete, and you are back at A, start the second round by stitching over the loops formed by the first row. As the circle decreases in size, so must the number of stitches. On this second round, work a buttonhole stitch in every other loop. Continue the rounds, decreasing the number of stitches as necessary on each alternate round to make the stitches lie flat on the fabric. To change threads, take the needle to the back of the work in the appropriate place, as indicated by B (2). Start a new thread by coming up again in the same hole, at B.

When the whole circle is filled, go down at C and finish off the yarn in the back by threading it through the wrong side of the chain stitches.

Variation. Work the same lacy buttonhole filling in a circle, which, when finished, will be removed from the background fabric. Start by couching the outlining threads to a backing. For a more finished look, these threads may be covered by close buttonhole stitches, as for the buttonholed bar (see fig. 2-122). Work the lacy filling stitches as described above, then snip the couching threads to free the piece from the backing.

To finish the loose end at C (2), bind it to a nearby loop with matching sewing thread. If the stitches are worked very close together, as for detached buttonhole stitch (fig. 2-4), loose ends may be woven back into the work on the wrong side.

Detached Buttonhole Filling with a Straight-Stitch Return (or *couching with buttonhole stitch*)

In this filling, the detached buttonhole stitch is worked only in one direction, from left to right. The return from right to left is made with a long straight stitch, just below the loops of the first row.

In traditional needle lace-making, when this stitch was worked very close together with no background showing, it was often referred to as the cloth, or toile stitch, the "cloth" referring to the very solid portion of the lace. When the stitches became more open and lacy, it was no longer cloth stitch. To make a sample, follow the directions for the first row of detached buttonhole filling, page 37.

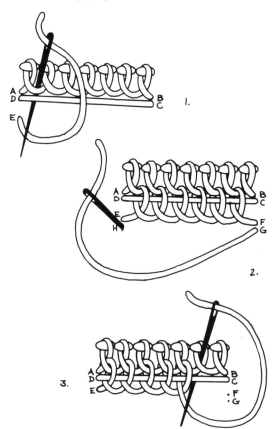

Figure 2-10. Detached buttonhole filling with straight-stitch return (or couching with buttonhole stitch).

For the second row, bring the needle and thread back up just below B at C (fig. 2-10, 1). From C lay a long straight stitch from right to left along the base of the previous row to D, just below A (1).

Come up at E (1) to start the third row. Again working the buttonhole stitch, slide the needle

from above, behind both the loop of the first row and the straight stitch of the second row. With the working thread under the needle tip, pull through gently. Complete the row by making a similar stitch between each of the stitches in the first row. End at F (2), by taking the needle and thread to the back of the work. Come up at G, returning again to H with a long straight stitch.

When the filling is complete, secure any loose ends of thread by weaving them into the wrong side of the anchoring stitches. Or, if the finished lace is to be removed from the backing, and the stitches are close together, weave the ends into the wrong side of the buttonhole stitches.

Variation. Thread the needle through the "eye" of each previous buttonhole stitch, rather than the loop (3). Or, try incorporating twigs, heavy-textured yarns, or ribbon along with the long straight stitch (fig. 2-11).

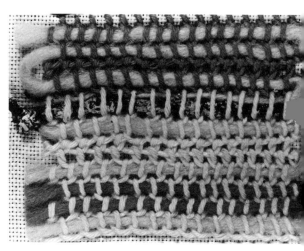

Figure 2-11. Couching with detached buttonhole stitch. The straight-stitch return is replaced by bulky yarn and a moss-covered twig.

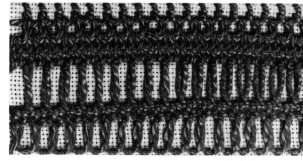

Figure 2-12. Detached buttonhole stitch with straight-stitch return. Worked in D.M.C. Perle Cotton size 3 on Hardanger cloth, alternating shallow and tight stitching with wide and open stitching.

Figure 2-13. Needle-lace medallion. The face and neck areas are detached buttonhole filling with a straight-stitch return. Courtesy of Beverly Rush.

Knotted Buttonhole Filling

Knotted buttonhole filling is a detached buttonhole stitch with an added knot at the base to hold it rigid. Because of this rigid nature, it is often not necessary to tack the last row of the finished net in place. This free edge forms a pocket, a place to put things in, or an area to stuff.

Work a row of backstitches as an anchor for the first row. Tie a knot in the end of the thread and bring the needle up at A (fig. 2-14, 1). Slide the needle, from above, under the first backstitch. Pull through and down to the right, over the working thread, making a loose buttonhole stitch. Now, slide the needle from left to right, behind the stitch just made. With the working thread under the tip of the needle, pull through to make the knot. (2)

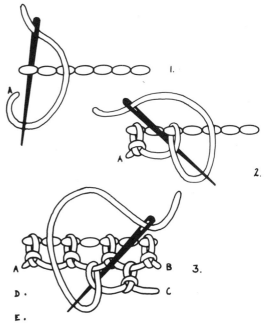

Figure 2-14. Knotted buttonhole filling.

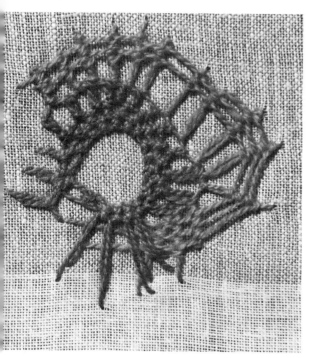

Figure 2-15. A circular shape made with four rows of knotted buttonhole filling, in a Swedish wool yarn, worked from the outside toward the center and bordered with raised chain band.

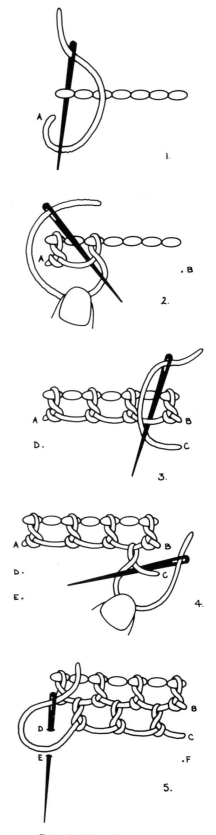

Figure 2-16. Venetian-point stitch.

In order to see the workings of the stitch more clearly, the diagram shows a knotted buttonhole stitch worked in every other backstitch. This way it may be very loose and open. Try it close together for a tight, textured look. Go down into the fabric to end the first row, at B (3).

For the return row, come up at C. Slide the needle, from above, behind the loop between the stitches in the first row. Pull through, over the working thread, to the left this time (3). Make the knot by sliding the needle from right to left, behind the stitch just made and over the working thread (3). Work a similar stitch in each loop, ending at the back of the work at D.

The rows may be continued indefinitely, changing thread as necessary at the beginning or end of any row.

Variation. For knotted buttonhole as an edging try the Antwerp edging (see fig. 2-47).

Venetian-Point Stitch

Venetian-point stitch was traditionally one of the buttonhole-stitch variations used in Venetian-point lace. Like knotted buttonhole filling, it is made with a single buttonhole stitch knotted at the base with another buttonhole stitch (see fig.

42

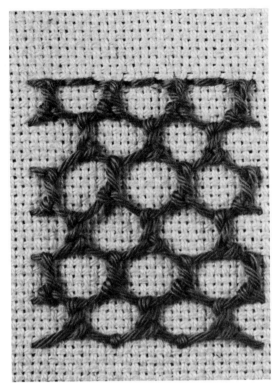

Figure 2-17. Sample of Venetian-point stitch.

2-14). To make the knot in the knotted but-tonhole stitch, the needle picks up both the threads at the base of the first buttonhole stitch. In the Venetian-point stitch the needle picks up only one thread.

To learn the stitch, first work a row of seven anchoring backstitches. With a knot at the end of the working thread, come up at A (fig. 2-16, 1), slightly below the end of the first backstitch. Looping the working thread counterclockwise, slide the needle from above, behind the first backstitch and out over the loop. Pull through gently to make the buttonhole stitch. Now, slide the needle from left to right behind the left, or lower, thread and over the right, or top, thread. Pull through to make a flat knot (2).

Continue working the stitches from left to right, with uniform loops between, in every sec-ond backstitch. You are spacing these stitches quite far apart in order to see how they work. Later, when they become a little more familiar to you, try working the stitches closer together, in every backstitch, with either coarser or finer thread.

End the first row by going down into the fabric at B (2). To begin the return row from right to left, come up again at C. C should be as far from B as B is from the top of the backstitches (3). Work a buttonhole stitch by sliding the needle, from above, behind the first loop between the stitches

in the first row, and out to the left over the work-ing thread (3). For the knot, slide the needle, from right to left this time, behind the right, lower, thread, and out over the left, top, thread (4). Work a stitch in each loop to complete the second row (5). Go down at D, then back up at E to begin the third row, a repeat of the first row.

When enough rows are finished, take the thread to the back of the work and then secure the end by working it into the wrong side of the anchoring stitches. A small tack over each loop in the last row will hold the finished mesh in place.

Double or Spaced Buttonhole Filling

Begin by enclosing the area to be filled with an outline of backstitch. The filling will be worked into this border only, being otherwise completely detached from the background fabric.

Tie a knot at the end of a length of thread, then bring needle and thread up at A (fig. 2-18, 1). Keeping the thread very loose and loopy, slide the needle, from above, behind the second back-stitch (B) at the top of the sample, without picking up any background fabric. Bring the needle out to the left, over the working thread, thus making a loose buttonhole stitch. Repeat this step behind the same backstitch, at B, to make a pair of but-tonhole stitches (2). Work two buttonhole stitches in every other backstitch (3, 4: C, D, E), until you come to the right-hand border. End this first row by sliding the needle under the second vertical backstitch, from left to right at F (4), with-out picking up any of the cloth.

Bring the needle back under the third back-stitch from right to left, G (4). To start the second row, work two buttonhole stitches over the loop between the stitches of the first row. Bring the needle over the working thread to the right this time. The stitches will immediately start forming a checkerboard or open-and-closed pattern (5).

As with all looped stitches, tension is very im-portant. Keep in mind the effect you are striving for. Double buttonhole can look entirely differ-ent if pulled tight with very loose loops between (6).

To hold the last row in place, hook the loops between stitches into the outlining backstitches (7).

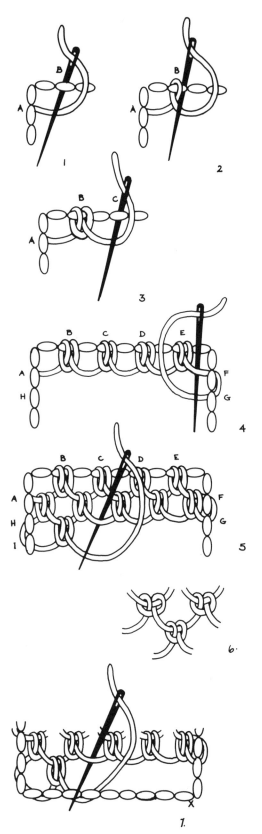

Figure 2-19. Traditional leaf shape encloses smaller leaf shapes of double buttonhole filling and buttonhole variations. Courtesy of The Costume and Textile Study Collection, School of Home Economics, University of Washington.

Figure 2-18. Double or spaced buttonhole filling.

44

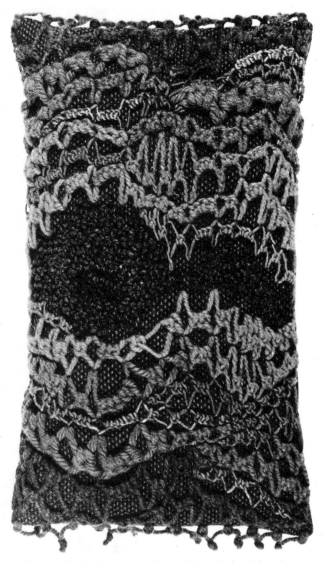

Figure 2-20. Random groups of spaced buttonhole stitches, in hand-dyed four-ply wool yarns, cover a pillow by Fritzi Oxley. The dark center area is rug-punched for added texture.

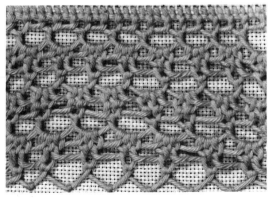

Figure 2-21. Spaced buttonhole stitches can make their own geometric patterns. Here rows of stitches alternate in groups of three, two, and one, and then back to three.

Figure 2-22. An elaborate diamond pattern of spaced buttonhole filling. For instructions, see Figure 2-23.

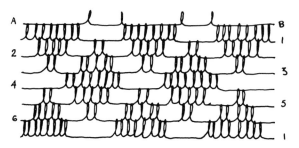

Figure 2-23. Diamond pattern of spaced buttonhole filling.

Variation. Spaced buttonhole filling may include groups of three, four, or more buttonhole stitches. Try a few of your own combinations.

Double Buttonhole Filling with a Straight-Stitch Return

This stitch is a simple variation of double buttonhole filling. Work pairs of stitches fairly tightly in one direction, with loose loops between, and then return with a long straight stitch.

Make a series of seven backstitches. Then with a knot in the end of the thread, bring the needle up at A (fig. 2-24, 1), below the first backstitch, to begin the first row. Slide the needle from above under the second backstitch and over the working thread. Pull through and down to the left. Work another stitch, exactly the same way, under the same backstitch. Pull through rather snugly this time (2). Work similar pairs of buttonhole stitches at C and D (3), keeping the loops between the pairs quite slack. End the first row by going down into the background fabric at E (3). Come up again at F (just below E) and return to G with a long straight stitch. Begin the buttonhole row again at H (4). Working from left to right, make pairs of stitches over each loop between the stitches of the first row, and the line F G (4 and 5). End the row at I (6). Alternate the first and second rows, each time returning to the left-hand border with a long straight stitch.

To keep the loops in place as you work, either insert straight pins at right angles to the loop (6), or work stitches around a ruler or smooth stick as a guide (7). Secure the last row as in Figure 2-4 (4 and 5).

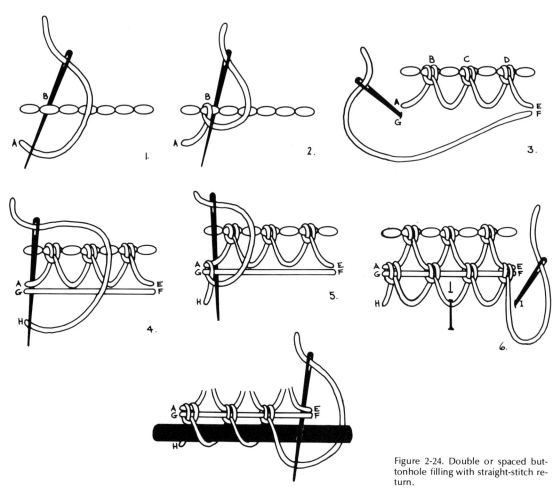

Figure 2-24. Double or spaced buttonhole filling with straight-stitch return.

Figure 2-25. Double buttonhole filling with loose loops between stitches and beads threaded on the straight-stitch return.

Knotted Double Buttonhole Filling

Six rows of double buttonhole filling with a single anchoring buttonhole stitch below make an intricate pattern in crochet cotton on a wool jersey dress (figs. 2-27 and 2-27a). Because the cut pattern pieces were narrow, and the fabric light weight and stretchy, the dress bodice was completely assembled before working the needle lace.

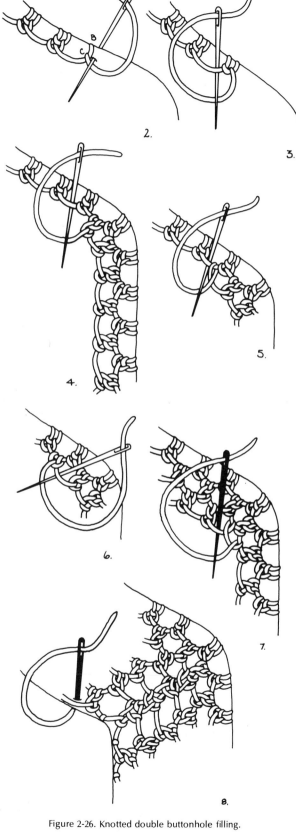

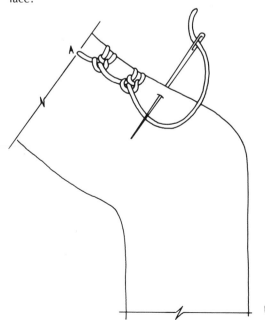

Figure 2-26. Knotted double buttonhole filling.

To begin, knot the end of the thread and come up in the shoulder seam, as indicated by A (fig. 2-26, 1). Working along the neck edge from left to right, make two buttonhole stitches, close together, by picking up a small amount of the background fabric at the top of the loop (1 and 2). To complete the stitch, work a single buttonhole stitch below the pair from left to right, picking up the looped thread only (3). Leaving about ½ inch between each group, finish the first row at the side seam, with a loose loop into the fabric in the same position as A (1).

To change thread at any time, go down into the background at point B (2), working several small stitches into the seam allowance. Then knot a new thread, come up at C (2), and continue.

Begin the second row at the side seam, stitching in the opposite direction, from right to left, back toward the shoulder. Work the same combination of stitches over each loop between the stitches in the first row (4, 5, and 6).

Where the pattern piece turns a corner it is necessary to decrease stitches. On the third row, worked in the same direction as the first, make a single buttonhole stitch in one loop, then another in the next. Then tie the two together with the usual single buttonhole worked below (7). In the same way, decrease by one stitch on the curve for each succeeding row. For a more pronounced curve it may be necessary to decrease by two stitches on each row.

Work enough rows to fill the inset piece. Finish off the last row by tacking the loops down with a row of small stitches on the seam line (8).

Variation. With this experiment as a guide, work out some other ideas. Look through clothing patterns — those with unique seaming automatically suggest design shapes to be filled with needle lace.

Figure 2-27. Wool-jersey dress with insets of knotted double buttonhole filling in crochet cotton.

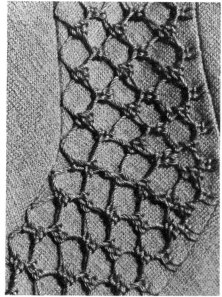

Figure 2-27a. Detail of inset in Figure 2-27.

Ceylon Stitch

Areas filled with Ceylon stitch look very much like the familiar stockinette stitch in knitting. It is usually worked only one way, from left to right. The working thread returns to the left-hand border behind the work, to begin each new row.

While working, be sure to keep the thread tension very loose, making each loop even slacker than you think it should be. The loops have a tendency to pop up, so use your left thumb to hold them in place as you go. Occasionally, it may be necessary to use straight pins or temporary small stitches into the background fabric to hold the row in place. Remove these later when the finished filling has been secured.

For a sample, knot the end of the thread and bring the needle and thread up at A (fig. 2-28, 1). Make seven very loose buttonhole stitches, catching the background fabric at the top of each loop to secure the first row. Go down into the fabric at B (2). Making a long diagonal straight stitch behind the work, come up at C (3) to begin the second row. Working again from left to right, slide the needle from right to left behind the cross of each stitch in the first row (3). Go down into the background at D (3), then take another long straight stitch across the back to E (4). Keeping the thread very loose and loopy, complete several more rows. Tack the last row in place by catching a few threads of the background fabric at the base of each loop (4), or by a series of small stitches (7).

Variation. There are many ways of varying Ceylon stitch. It can be made very open and ladder-like (5, 6, 7) or made heavy and textured by returning to the left-hand border with another set of loops worked over the first (8).

While experimenting, I discovered how to make a hole in the filling, a technique that works well for any of the detached buttonhole stitches. To make a "hole" sample, begin as for plain Ceylon stitch with seven stitches across. Work three rows. On the fourth row, work two stitches, then skip three, leaving a long thread or bar. Complete the remaining two stitches. Take the thread to the back of the work as usual. For the fifth row, again work the first two stitches, then work the next three over the bar made by the previous row. Work the last two stitches. To finish, add two more plain rows, tacking down the last row to secure the finished sample.

Try one hole. Then, perhaps make a small stitchery with several holes, varying their position, size, and the thickness of the thread.

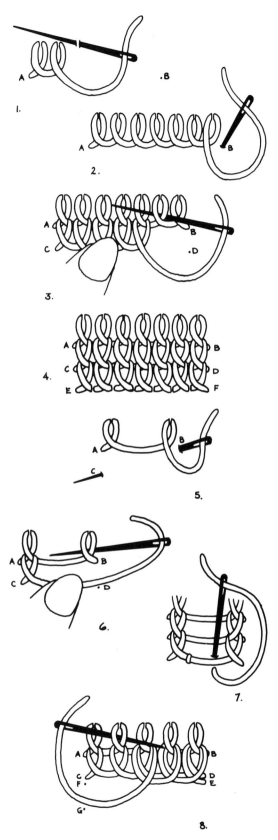

Figure 2-28. Ceylon stitch.

49

Figure 2-29. Ceylon stitch worked in both directions to make a double thread.

Figure 2-30. Ceylon stitch worked to produce an empty central space, or "hole" in the net.

Detached Up-and-Down Buttonhole Filling

Detached up-and-down buttonhole filling is a very close relative of double buttonhole filling, but is made with a pair of buttonhole stitches, one right-side-up and one upside-down.

Working on a loosely woven background fabric, knot the end of the thread and bring the needle and thread up at A (fig. 2-31, 1). Work a single buttonhole stitch, picking up a few threads of the background at the top of the loop B (1).

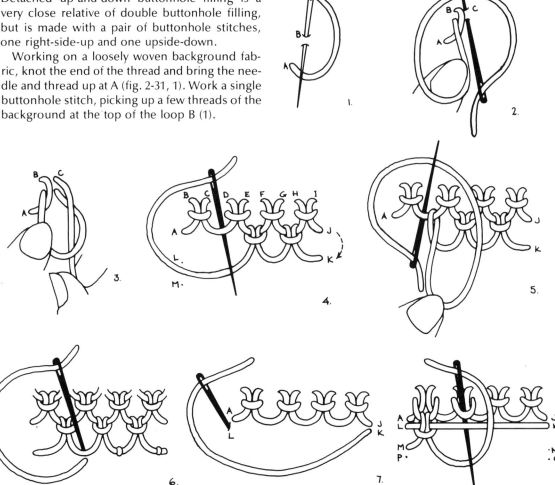

Figure 2-31. Detached up-and-down buttonhole filling.

Now, holding the working thread in place with your left thumb, arrange the remainder, clockwise, over the work, in a large upside-down U (2). To complete the stitch, insert the needle into the background fabric from below, coming out at C (2) and over the working thread. Pull through and down gently, keeping your left thumb on the loop as long as possible (3).

Leaving even spaces between, work similar pairs of stitches at D E, F G, and H I (4). Go down into the fabric at J (4) coming up again at K (4), to begin the return row.

This time the pairs of stitches are worked from right to left, over the loop between the stitches in the first row (4 and 5). End the second row at L (4), coming up again at M (4) to begin the third row, a repeat of the first row.

When enough rows have been completed, secure each loop of the last row to the background with a separate row of stitches (6).

Variation. Work the first row in the usual way, and then return to the left-hand border with a long straight stitch K L (7). Begin the third row at M (8), this time working the two buttonhole stitches into the middle of each stitch of the first row, and behind the thread K L. Finish the row at N (8), returning to the left-hand border with another straight stitch from O to P. Continue, repeating the first and second rows.

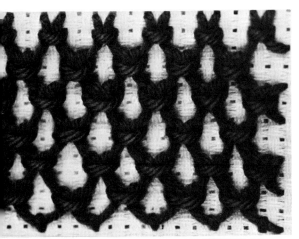

Figure 2-32. Sample of detached up-and-down buttonhole filling.

Figure 2-33. Sample of detached up-and-down buttonhole-filling variation: Stitches worked in one direction with a straight-stitch return, and succeeding rows worked back into the stitch rather than the loop between.

Valsesian Stitch

Valsesian stitch developed in Italy as a detached, loosely knotted, textured filling for the needle-made lace called Puncetto work. In Figure 2-34, the stitches are widely spaced to show their structure, but the result is far more successful when the stitches are close together and in shallow rows.

To make a sample, work a row of seven backstitches. Knot the end of the thread, then bring the needle up at A (fig. 2-34, 1). Arrange the working thread in a wide loop to the left and above the work. Hold the needle in the right hand, then working from above, slide it behind the first backstitch. With the left hand, wrap the working thread snugly over and then under the tip of the needle, holding it firmly in place with the left thumb (1). Pull the needle and thread through to form a loose knot (2).

To help keep an even tension, draw an imaginary line between A and B. The knotted lower edge of each finished stitch should touch this line.

Continue toward the right-hand border, repeating the first step (1) in each backstitch. Take the thread to the back of the work at B, then up again at C (3).

For the return row, arrange the working thread in a counter-clockwise loop below the work, holding the left side with the left thumb (4). Slide the needle vertically between the last two stitches of the previous row, behind the top of the looped working thread, and out over the bottom of the looped working thread. Pull through to form the knot. Continue from right to left, working a stitch in each space between the stitches of the first row (5).

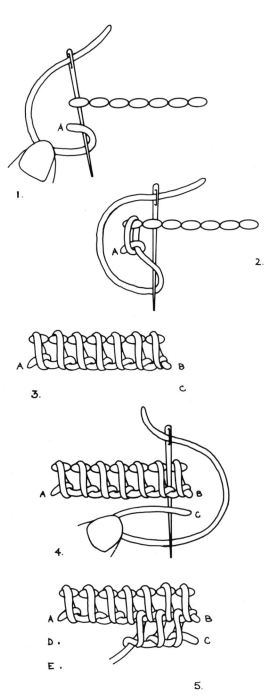

Figure 2-34. Valsesian stitch.

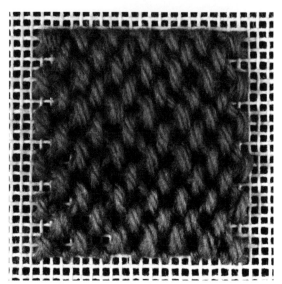

Figure 2-35. Sample of Valsesian stitch.

At the left border of the work, go down at D, then come up again at E (5). Repeat the first and second rows several times to become familiar with the stitch. As you work, the net will have a tendency to arch in the middle. When the last row is finished, pull the arch into a horizontal position by tacking the lower edge to the background with a separate row of small stitches (see fig. 2-4, 5).

Tulle Stitch, or Whipped Lace-Stitch Filling

The tulle stitch, which is a version of the lace-stitch filling, is worked only from left to right, with a whipping or overcasting stitch used for returning the thread to the left side. In lace-stitch filling, the initial row is the same as tulle stitch (fig. 2-36) and the return row, instead of being whipped, is the reverse of the initial row. The terms tulle stitch and whipped lace stitch are interchangeable, and are both used in reference material on needle lace.

Outline the area to be filled by a row of backstitch or chain stitch. To begin, bring the needle and thread out at A, (fig. 2-36, 1). Arrange the working thread in a loose S-shaped curve, holding it in place with the left thumb. Working from above, slide the needle behind the second backstitch at the top of the design, being careful not to pick up any of the background fabric. The needle will first go over, then under the working thread you are holding (1). When using a yarn that does not slide easily take up the slack in the S-curve by pulling it snugly against the needle. Pull the thread through, but not too tightly, to form the twist.

Work a second tulle stitch in the same manner in the fourth backstitch at C (2), keeping the tension loose. Continue across to the right-hand

Opposite
Above: Happiness Is, a textured hanging in spiderweb techniques, by Helen W. Richards. Photo by artist. Below: *India: Summer* (detail), a work combining various needle-lace and detached stitches, by Karin Morris.

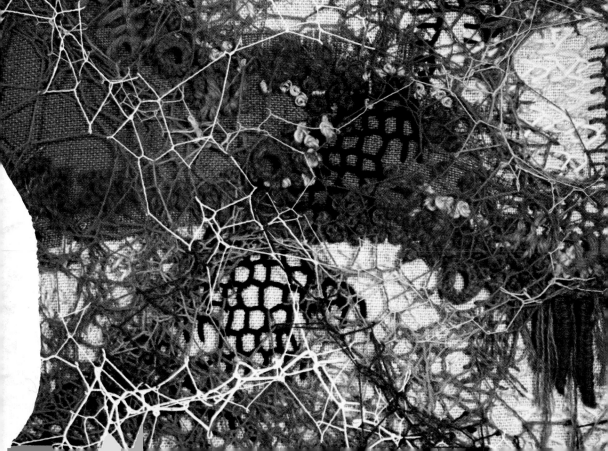

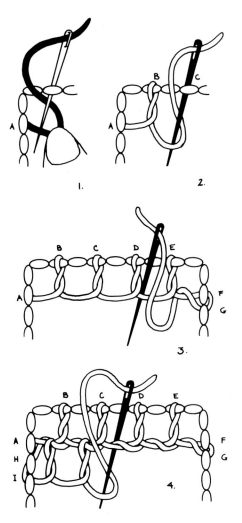

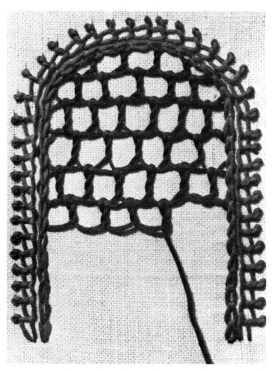

Figure 2-37. Tulle stitch or whipped lace-stitch filling in an arch of chain stitches. The outline is surface embroidery in crested chain stitch.

Figure 2-36. Tulle stitch or whipped lace-stitch filling.

border, slide the needle from left to right under the second backstitch at F, and then go back under the third backstitch, from right to left, at G.

Return the working thread to the left-hand border by working a whipping stitch in each loop between the stitches of the previous row (3). This line may be pulled taut, easing the tulle stitches along it with the tip of the needle as you go. Secure the whipping thread at the left border by sliding the needle from right to left under the third backstitch at H. Bring the needle and thread back under the fourth backstitch, from left to right, at I.

You are now ready to start the second row of tulle stitches (4). Continue working the rows as before (1, 2, 3) until the entire space is filled. The loops of the last row may be caught and secured by the outlining stitches (see fig. 2-18, 7), or tacked in place with some tiny stitches.

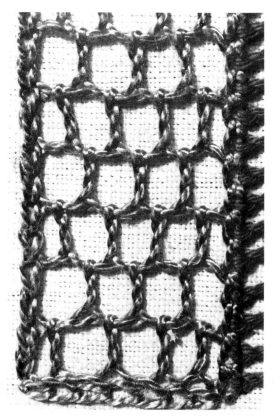

Figure 2-38. Tulle stitch attached to an outline of chain stitch.

Hollie Stitch

Hollie stitch dates back to the Middle Ages when it was used to work the background in Holy Point needle-made laces for the church. It is made with a twisted buttonhole stitch, worked close together and only from left to right, and then returning to the left-hand border with a long straight stitch. Traditionally a pattern of holes was made in the tightly stitched geometric designs by occasionally skipping a few stitches and then picking them up again on the next row.

To make a sample, work a series of backstitches as an anchor for the first row. Knot the end of the working thread and come up at A (fig. 2-39, 1). The distance from A to B determines the height of the stitches. For fine, shallow rows, A should be close to B; for heavy, deep rows, farther apart.

Wrap the working thread counterclockwise around the left index finger — under, over, under (1) — then carefully slide the finger out so the loop maintains its shape. Slide the needle from above behind the first backstitch (B), behind the top of the loop, and out over the crossed threads at the base of the loop (2). Before pulling the needle through, tighten the twist around the needle by pulling the working thread firmly to the right (3). Put the left index finger on the twist to hold it in place, then pull the needle through. If necessary, adjust the finished stitch by holding the working thread taut with the left hand, while at the same time pulling up on the loop at B (4) with the needle in the right hand.

Work a hollie stitch over each backstitch at C, D, E, F, G and H (5), going down into the fabric at I to complete the first row. Come up again just below I at J, working a long straight stitch to K (5), from right to left.

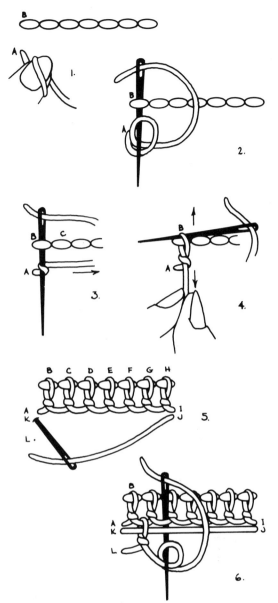

Figure 2-39. Hollie stitch.

Come up at L to begin the second row of hollie stitches. To insure even rows, L should be the same distance from A as A is from B. To work the stitches in the second row, slide the needle from above, behind each loop between the stitches of the first row, behind the long straight stitch, and through the loop in the working thread (6).

When enough rows are completed, finish off the thread by weaving it into the anchoring stitches on the wrong side of the work. To hold the last row in place, tack the loops between the stitches to the background fabric as in detached buttonhole filling.

Figure 2-40. Sample of hollie stitch in two colors.

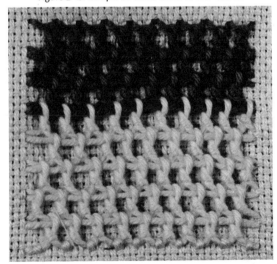

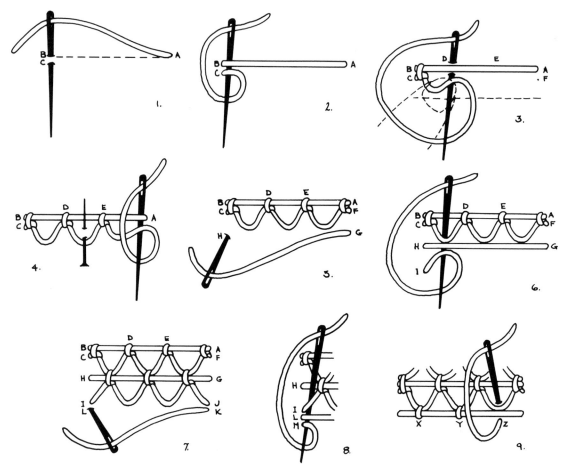

Figure 2-41. Diamond filling.

Diamond Filling

Diamond filling is an open, diamond-shaped mesh worked from left to right with loops and coral knots, and then back, from right to left, with a long straight stitch. Keeping the loops even may be difficult at first, but by using your left thumb or a straight pin to hold each one in place as you go, the technique will soon develop.

To make a sample, knot the thread and come up at A (fig. 2-41, 1). Count threads to measure equal spaces on the background fabric to determine the distance between each stitch and the total length of the line A B. The finished sample (fig. 2-42) is on basket-weave monkscloth with six threads between each stitch, making the total length from A to B 36 counted threads. Go down to the back of the work at B and come up just below, at C (1), in a position to begin the first row of knotted loops. Arrange the working thread in a clockwise loop. Slide the needle from above, behind the line A B, behind the top of the loop, and

pull through over the bottom of the loop to make a knot (2).

For the first and last knots on the first row, the needle need not enter the background fabric. However, in order to keep the line A B from sagging in the middle, it is a good idea to pick up a thread or two of the cloth as you work the knots at D and E (4). The succeeding rows will all be completely detached, hooking into the background only at both ends.

For the finished net to look right, the loops in between each coral knot must each be the same depth. The horizontal dotted line (3) indicates a guide for the finished loop. This is an imaginary line marked only by the weave of the fabric, but it may help at first to draw it in with a temporary line of basting stitches.

Arrange the first loop so it is a little above the guideline, and hold it firmly in place with your left thumb while working the second knot at D

(3). The loop will slacken and drop into position with its base along the guideline after the knot is tightened.

Continue, from left to right, working the third knot at E, and the fourth at the end of the line at A (4). Go down into the background fabric just below A at F (5).

Hold the finished loops flat with straight pins (4). To keep the working thread from catching in the pins, remove them one at a time as you work the next row.

Come up at G (5), returning to the left-hand border with a long straight stitch along the base of the loops. Go down to the back of the work at H. To begin the second row of knotted loops, come up at I (6). I should be the same distance below H as C is above H. Work the first knot by again arranging the working thread in a clockwise loop and holding it in place with your left thumb. Slide the needle from above, behind the loop of the first row, behind the line G H, and behind the top of the looped working thread. Be careful not to pick up any background fabric. Pull through and down over the bottom of the looped working thread to form the knot (6). Finish the row, from left to right, by working knots over the loops between D and E and between E and A, each time tying in the three threads. End the row at the back of the work at J (7). Come up again at K, carrying the long straight stitch to the left again and down at L (7).

To begin the third row of knotted loops, come up at M (8), just below L. Make the first knot as for Row one (2), but this time tie in all three threads. Continue the third row as for the first row, to the right-hand border.

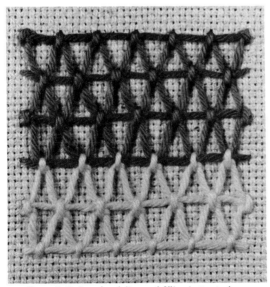

Figure 2-42. Sample of diamond filling in two colors.

When you have completed enough rows of the diamond filling, anchor the loops of the last row and the long straight stitch by a series of small stitches into the background fabric at X, Y, and Z (9).

Filet Stitch

Filet stitch is much like the diamond-filling stitch, being made up of a series of loops tied together with coral knots. However, in filet stitch the knotted loops are usually worked diagonally in both directions, rather than horizontally in only one direction.

Filet stitch is a detached embroidery stitch made with a tapestry needle and a single thread. It imitates filet lace or netting, which is made with a continuous thread on a netting needle. This tool is rather like a small version of a weaver's shuttle. Traditionally, when the knotted mesh of filet lace was completed, areas were filled in or embroidered with another thread, using simple over-and-under weaving or combinations of looped stitches.

There are numerous references to filet stitch, each describing slight variations in technique. In the diagram, I have illustrated the method of working the stitch that best resembles filet lace. A simpler method of making a filet-like knotted grid as a base for other filling stitches is shown in figure 2-78.

In working the traditional filet stitch it is important to learn how to make each loop the same size. Uneven loops will produce lopsided squares and an untidy finished grid. Use the left thumb and straight pins whenever possible to make the job easier.

To make a sample, first decide on the size of each square and the total area to be filled. Then outline it with a contrasting basting thread (fig. 2-43, 6). Knot the end of the thread and come up at A (1), A should be as far from the top left-hand corner as the length of one side of one square. Go down at B, diagonally across from A, leaving the thread a little slack.

Come up at C (2), which should be as far from B as B is from the upper left corner. With the tip of the needle, pull down on the line A B to make a right angle, and hold it in place with the left thumb. Arrange the working thread in a loose diagonal from C that meets the right angle and then slide the left thumb over to hold both threads. Then, with the working thread looped clockwise, slide the needle from above and diagonally to the right, behind both threads, and

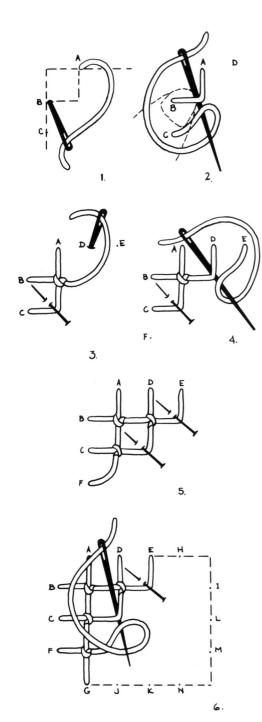

Figure 2-43. Filet stitch.

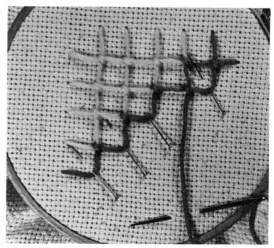

Figure 2-44. Sample of filet stitch being worked on monkscloth stretched in an embroidery hoop. Straight pins keep the net in place as the stitching progresses.

this time arrange the working thread in a counter-clockwise loop (4). Go down to the back of the work at F (5), to end the third row.

When enough rows are completed to fill in the left side of the marked space, begin the return row at the lower edge (6:G). Work toward the top right, as for C to D. Continue filling the space with knotted squares, ending at the back of the work at N (6). Finish off the thread on the wrong side by wrapping it several times around the back of one of the anchoring stitches. Or, for a free-hanging open mesh, weave loose threads into the supporting edge of braid, cord, or fabric at the end of any row.

Figure 2-45. Baby pillowcase with insert of filet lace. Flower motifs are a woven filling over the net base. Courtesy of Patricia A. Lantz.

out over the loop to make the knot (2). Keep the thumb securely on the work until the knot is tightened. With a straight pin pull the loose diagonal from C into a right angle, and pin in place (3). Work another loose diagonal stitch from the first knot to D (3).

Come up at E (4) to begin the third diagonal row. Make a knot (2) around each right angle, but

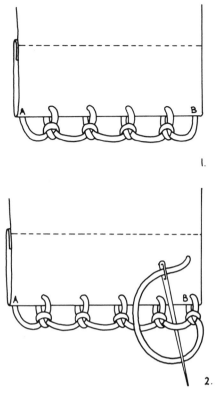

Figure 2-46. Traditional needle lace. Areas outlined with tape or braid are filled with filet stitch, buttonhole stitches, and woven spiderwebs. Courtesy of Ada King.

EDGING STITCHES

Antwerp-Edging Stitch

Antwerp-edging stitch is a knotted buttonhole stitch used to decorate an edge rather than to fill an area. The edge to be decorated should either be a selvage or a finished hem. This makes a strong base to stitch into, whereas a raw edge may pull out or show through between stitches.

Following the directions for knotted buttonhole filling on page 41, begin by slipping the needle and thread into the open end of the hem, and out in the fold at 2-47, A (1). Work evenly spaced knotted buttonhole stitches from left to right, catching both layers of fabric, to the end of the hem B (1). For a single row, finish the thread off at B by stitching into the fold, between the two fabric layers, and out to the back of the work. Take a few small stitches in the underside of the hem.

Add a second row in one of two ways. If you have ample thread left by the time you reach B, and the distance back to A is not too great, reverse directions and work another row of knotted buttonhole stitches from right to left. Finish off

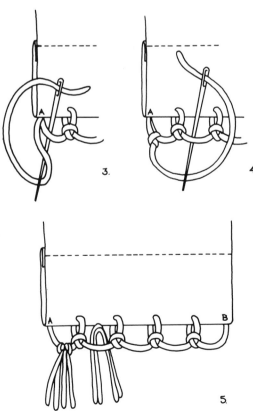

Figure 2-47. Antwerp edging stitch.

59

the thread in the fold at A (2). Or, if you need a new length of thread, knot the end and begin again in the same hole as A. Work a coral knot (3) to anchor the thread to the first loop. Then proceed with knotted buttonhole stitches in each loop of the previous row (4). End the thread at B, working a coral knot on the loop, before going up into the hem.

For a wide band, add many rows or a fringe between the loops (5).

Braid-Edging Stitch

For a simple, knotted, decorative edging to a finished hem, try the braid edging. It can be made in a single row or, for a more elaborate trim, in multiple rows (fig. 2-48, 8).

Tie a knot in the end of the thread, then slide the needle inside the open end of the finished hem, and out in the fold at A (1). Make a loop

around your thumb (2) by wrapping the working thread clockwise, first over, and then under. Slide the thumb out carefully so as to maintain the loop, and then insert the needle from below through the loop, behind the fabric fold, and out at B (3). Place the working thread around the tip of the needle, then tighten the loop around the base of the needle (4). Pull through and up (5), then down, to anchor the stitch in place (6).

Continue evenly spaced stitches, with even loops between, at C, D, and E, to the end of the hem (7). Finish off the thread at F by threading the needle into the folded edge between the two fabric layers and then out to the wrong side of the work. Secure the end by taking a few stitches into the back of the fabric.

Variation. Try laced insertion, where two finished edges are joined by lacing or whipping braid edges together (see fig. 2-61).

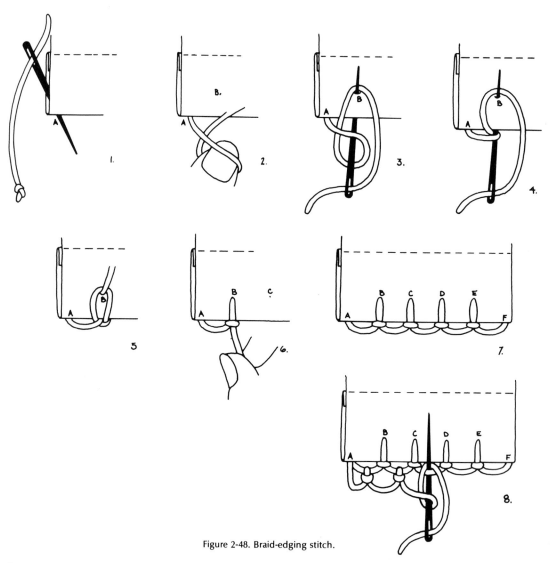

Figure 2-48. Braid-edging stitch.

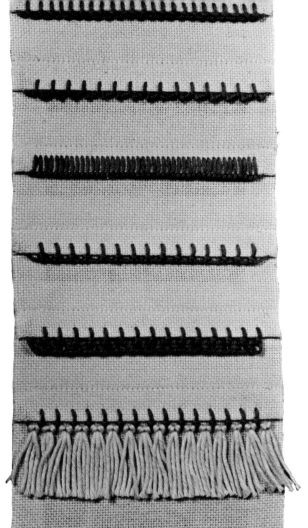

Figure 2-49. Sample of edging stitches. *From top to bottom:* braid edging, Armenian edging, plaited edging, Antwerp edging, double row of Antwerp edging and single row of Antwerp edging with added fringe.

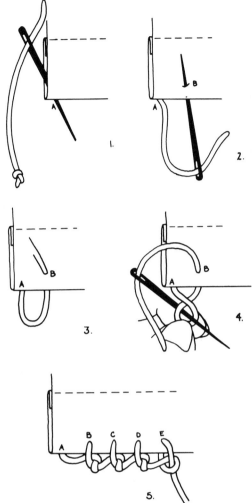

Figure 2-50. Armenian-edging stitch.

Armenian-Edging Stitch

For a scroll-like edge to a finished hem, use the Armenian-edging stitch (fig. 2-50). Prepare the fabric for a sample by folding and pressing a 1-inch hem to the wrong side, either pinning or machine stitching it in place.

Tie a knot in the end of the working thread, then slide the needle inside the hem and out at A (1) in the crease of the fold. Pull the thread through to hide the knot in the hem.

Now, slide the needle from below, behind the folded edge, and up through the two fabric layers at B (2). Pull through, but not all the way, leaving an approximately ¾-inch long loop (3). Twist the loop with the left hand, crossing A over B (4). Holding the base of the loop firmly, slide the needle through it from the left, under the left side, and out over the right (4). Pull the working

thread all the way through while still holding the loop. Tighten the knot against the fabric edge.

Continue along the edge from left to right, working evenly spaced stitches at C, D, and E (5). At the right-hand border, finish off the thread as for braid-edging stitch (fig. 2-48), or Antwerp edging (fig. 2-47).

Plaited-Edging Stitch

Plaited-edging stitch (fig. 2-51) can be decorative trim for a hemmed edge or a way of binding a raw edge. On a folded edge the stitches may be as close together or far apart as you wish, but to cover a raw edge, they must be very close together.

To make a sample on a folded edge, knot the end of the thread, then slide the needle between the fabric layers and out in the fold line (1). Begin

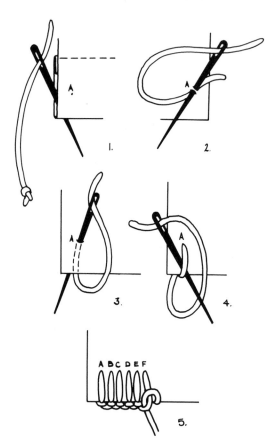

Figure 2-52. Patchwork vest of wool double-knit fabric, joined by Italian-buttonhole insertion, by the author.

Figure 2-51. Plaited-edging stitch.

the first stitch (3) by threading the needle through both layers of fabric at A (1).

To cover a raw edge the thread must first be secured on the wrong side of the work at A (2). Take two very small stitches into a single thread in the background fabric, which will not show through to the front.

Turn the work to the right side and begin the edging by threading the needle through the single layer of fabric at A (3). Pull through and down to tighten the stitch. For the second step, work a detached knot by sliding the needle from left to right, between the stitch just made and the fabric background. Pull through and down over the looped working thread (4).

Repeat the last two steps, making close stitches to hide the raw edge (5). At the right-hand border, finish off the thread on the wrong side (2). For a folded edge, thread the needle back up through the fold line, between the two fabric layers, and out to the back of the work. Take a few small stitches in the wrong side of the fabric.

INSERTION STITCHES

Insertion stitches decoratively join two pieces of fabric by filling a narrow space between the finished edges with detached stitches.

Traditionally, braids, either machine- or bobbin-made (see fig. 1-13) were joined together with needle lace and insertion stitches. To hold the braids in place, they were first basted to a heavy paper marked with a pattern and then backed with a double layer of fabric. When the spaces enclosed by the braid were completely filled, the basting was snipped between the fabric layers, and the finished piece fell free from the backing.

From this technique, I evolved the idea for the vest in Figure 2-52. An appliquéd patchwork of double-knit wool is substituted for the braid. To make this vest, first draw the vest pattern on muslin with a permanent waterproof felt pen. Then, cut pieces of the knit fabric to fill the pattern area, pinning them to the muslin backing with their edges touching. Appliqué the pieces to the muslin with basting or blind stitch (see fig. 1-18), using the needle to turn each edge under ¼ inch. When the appliqué is finished, there should be a ½-inch space between all pieces, which can be filled with any decorative insertion. The model has Italian buttonhole (see below) done in a Swedish two-ply wool yarn. As you work, be careful not to stitch into the muslin backing, but only into the edges of the patchwork pieces. Ends of threads may be taken to the back of the work to be woven in later. When the insertion stitches are completed, clip the appliqué basting and remove the muslin backing. Line the finished patchwork front with a soft fabric if you wish. Then machine stitch shoulder and side seams to a solid-color back. Bind the neck, armholes, and hem with a knit-fabric· trim.

Italian-Buttonhole Insertion

An ornate-looking stitch, the Italian-buttonhole insertion is simply a combination of two basic stitches—buttonhole and Cretan (see figs. 2-4 and 2-70). The first few steps may feel awkward but, as you work, a pattern and rhythm will develop.

Make a sample by basting two pieces of fabric, finished edges together, to a fairly stiff fabric or paper backing, leaving about ½ to ¾ inch of backing showing between the finished fabric edges. This is the space for stitching (fig. 2-53, 1). Knot the end of the working thread, then with a small tapestry needle, slide in between the edges of the fold and up at A (1), about ⅛ inch from the fold. Pull the thread through. With the working thread above the needle, cross over to B (2) and take a small stitch from the front through both layers of the folded edge. Pull the thread fairly taut, making a bar between A and B (3). Work four buttonhole stitches over the bar (3 and 4). Work a Cretan stitch at C (4) into the right-hand edge, then cross back to the left, working a similar Cretan stitch at D (5), slightly below C.

Now you are ready for another group of buttonhole stitches. Cross back to the right side by working four buttonhole stitches over the Cretan stitch to C (6). Anchor this group of stitches by working another Cretan stitch at E (7). Swing back toward D with four more buttonhole stitches, working each time from the center to the edge (8). Then again anchor the thread with a Cretan stitch at F (9).

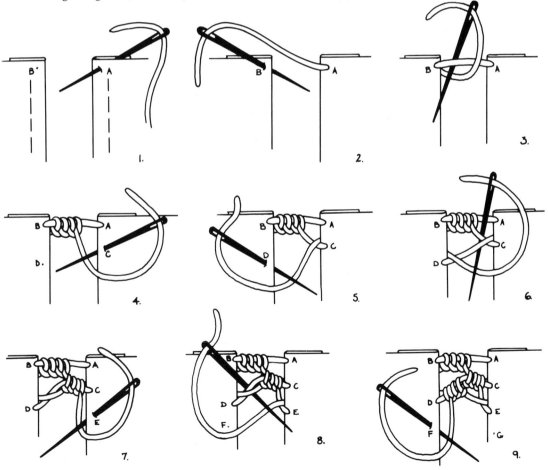

Figure 2-53. Italian-buttonhole insertion.

Continue alternating sides, completing on each side four buttonhole stitches and an anchoring Cretan stitch. When you need to change thread, leave the end loose or take it through to the back of the work, to be woven in after the finished piece is removed from the backing. Begin a new thread by concealing the knot in the fold of the appliquéd piece.

Buttonholed Half-Bar Insertion

A full buttonholed bar is a single thread or groups of threads, attached to the background at both ends, and then completely covered with buttonhole stitches worked very close together. The buttonholed half-bar insertion is a horizontal thread that joins two finished edges, but is only half covered with buttonhole stitches (fig. 2-54).

Begin by basting the pieces to be joined to a stiff paper or fabric background, leaving ½ to ¾ inch of backing showing between. The measurement depends on the weight of your yarn and the number of buttonhole stitches per bar.

Slide the needle and thread inside the open end of the finished hem. Come up in the fold at A (1). Cross over, from left to right, to B (1), and take a small vertical stitch in the fold from B to C.

Pull the thread through firmly, making the horizontal (A to B) fairly taut. Work back toward A, from right to left and over the bar A B, with a series of three to five buttonhole stitches (2 and 3) that cover a little less than half the base thread. Make the next bar by taking a small vertical stitch in the fold from D to E, slightly below C (3). Pull through, and again work the same number of buttonhole stitches, but this time from left to right, toward the center of the space (4).

Alternate first the bar and then the evenly spaced buttonhole stitches between each finished edge at F G and H I (5). End the series at J (5) by threading the needle into the fold opposite A, between the two fabric layers, and out to the back of the work. After the backing is removed, anchor any loose ends by working several small stitches in the wrong side of the fabric. Experiment with these half bars to see what they look like in fine thread with fewer buttonhole stitches on each horizontal bar, in a narrower or wider space, or in a heavy thread with more buttonhole stitches on each horizontal bar.

Variation. Substitute two rows of backstitch for the folded fabric edges; work the insertion between the backstitches for a rich braidlike trim.

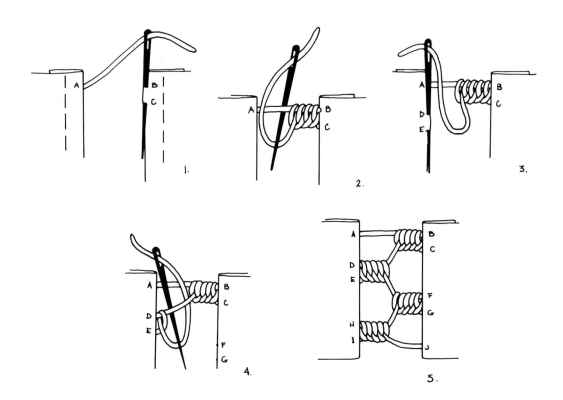

Figure 2-54. Buttonholed half-bar insertion.

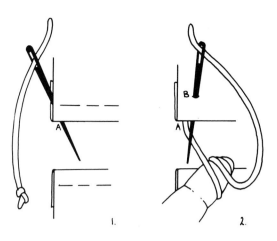

Buttonhole Insertion

Buttonhole insertion is evenly spaced groups of buttonhole stitches that alternate from side to side between two finished fabric edges. Ordinary buttonhole stitch may be used, but Figure 2-55 shows a stronger, more decorative version that is knotted in place by an extra twist of the thread.

As previously, baste the folded edges of two pieces of fabric to a stiff paper or fabric backing leaving ½ inch of backing showing. Beginning at the upper left edge, knot the end of the thread, and then slide the needle between the two fabric layers of the upper hem and out in the fold at A (1). Working from above, go down through the two layers of fabric at B (2), being careful not to pick up any of the backing. Before pulling the needle through, place the working thread behind the needle. Then make a loop by winding it over, under, then over the left index finger (2). Carefully slide this loop over the end of the needle (3). Take in the slack by tightening the knot on the needle as far as it will go (4). Pull through to form a knotted stitch. Complete the group of four (5:C, D, E).

Move to the lower edge and insert the needle from below, at F (5), through both layers of the fabric. With the working thread behind the tip of the needle, wrap the thread behind the needle and around the left index finger, this time under, over, under (5). Gently move the finger to the left and up, dropping the loop over the point of the needle (6). Tighten the knot and hold it in place with your finger while pulling the needle through (7). Work similar stitches at G, H and I (8), then begin the second upper series at J (8). Complete the upper group at K, L, and M (9), repeating the steps shown in Diagrams 2 through 4, for each stitch.

Continue filling the horizontal space with these groups of stitches, working alternately from the upper to the lower edge and back to the upper. To finish off or change a thread, poke the needle

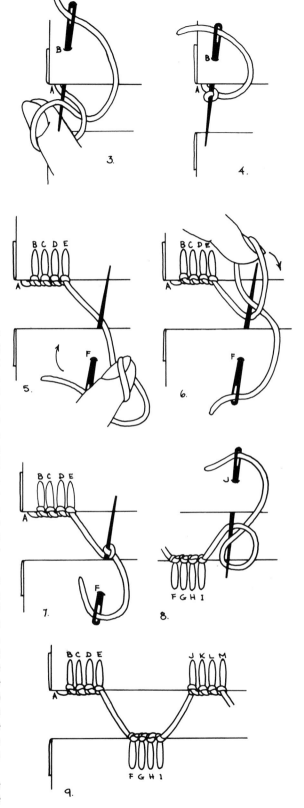

Figure 2-55. Buttonhole insertion.

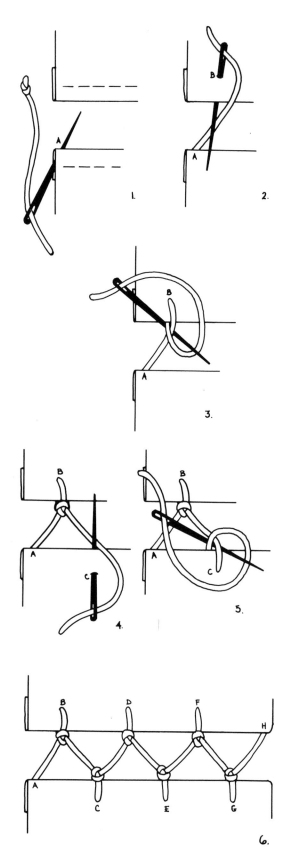

into the fold, between the two fabric layers of the hem, and out through the backing. When the insertion is finished and the backing removed, weave the loose ends of thread into the wrong side of the buttonhole stitches or take a few small tacks in the wrong side of the fabric.

Variation. Try other samples with different threads, increasing or decreasing the number of stitches in each group, working the groups closer together or farther apart, or widening or narrowing the space between the fabric edges.

Knotted Insertion

Knotted insertion is a knotted buttonhole filling (see fig. 2-14) used to join two finished edges by working alternately from one edge to the other. It may be open and airy in a fine linen thread, with wide spaces between stitches, or close and textured in a three-ply wool yarn, with narrow spaces between stitches.

After basting the two fabric edges to a stiff paper or cloth backing, knot the end of the thread and then come up into the lower fold and out at A (fig. 2-56, 1). Working from above, insert the needle at B (2) through both layers of the upper finished edge and out between the fabric and the backing. Pull through and down, over the working thread. To make the knot, loop the working thread around counterclockwise, slide the needle from left to right behind the base of the stitch, and pull through over the working thread (3).

Work another buttonhole stitch on the lower edge at C (4) but to make the knot, this time, loop the working thread clockwise. Slide the needle behind the stitch and over the loop, and pull through (5). Repeat (2, 3, 4, 5) to fill the entire space (6). Finish off the thread at H (6) by stitching through the fold, between the two layers of fabric, and out to the back of the work. Let the thread end dangle until the finished piece is removed from the backing. Then rethread the needle and take a few tiny stitches in the wrong side of the work.

Twisted Insertion, or Faggoting

Twisted insertion stitch, or faggoting, as it is sometimes known, is a method of joining two fabric pieces by working diagonally back and forth over an open space. A good rule to remember is that each time a stitch is taken, the needle goes behind the finished edge; each time a twist is made, the needle goes behind the finished stitch.

Figure 2-56. Knotted insertion.

To hold the work in place, baste the edges to be joined to a stiff-paper or fabric backing, ½ inch apart, so that the backing shows through.

Working from left to right, begin by tying a knot in the thread, and then coming up inside the fold and out at A (fig. 2-58, 1). Cross over diagonally, under the upper finished edge and up through both layers of fabric at B (1), to make the first stitch. Now, for the twist, slide the needle from the right, behind the stitch A B (2). Move the needle tip to the right, behind the lower edge, and up through both layers of fabric at C (3). Pull through firmly to adjust the twist. For the lower twist, again slide the needle from the right and behind the stitch just made (3). Swing the needle tip to the right, under the upper edge, and pull through at D (3).

Fill the entire open space, working the twisted insertion back and forth at E, F, G, H and I (4). To change or end a thread, finish off at J (4) by stitching through the fold, between the two layers of fabric, and out through the backing. Begin a new thread the same way, only from the backing through to the top of the work. Leave the loose ends to be woven in later when the backing is removed.

Figure 2-57. Sampler, of insertion stitches. *From top to bottom:* buttonholed half-bar insertion, buttonhole insertion, knotted insertion, twisted insertion (or faggoting), and Cretan-stitch insertion.

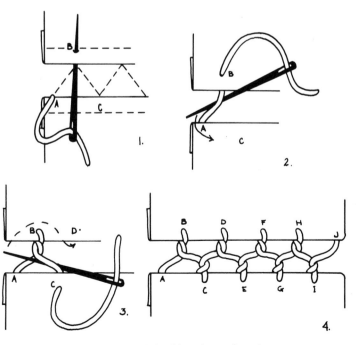

Figure 2-58. Twisted insertion, or faggoting.

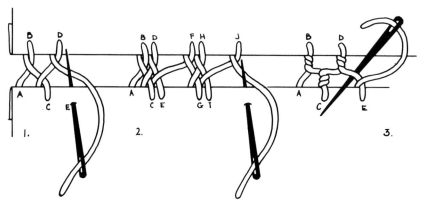

Figure 2-59. Cretan-stitch insertion.

Cretan-Stitch Insertion

A Cretan stitch (see fig. 2-70) is worked either vertically, from top to bottom, or horizontally, from left to right. The stitches may be spaced singly or in groups, far apart or close together, twisted or plain.

Figure 2-59 shows three ways to use Cretan stitch as an insertion. Placing the stitches close together will make a braidlike ridge, farther apart will make a delicate open border. Let these ideas be just a beginning for your further experiments.

For a sample, baste the two finished edges of the fabric firmly to a backing, ½ inch apart so the backing shows through, knot the end of the thread, and come up inside the lower fold at A (1). Insert the needle from above at B, stitching through both layers of the fabric but not into the backing. Pull through and down over the working thread. Now, again insert the needle from below at C, picking up only the folded edge. Pull through and up over the working thread. Repeat the stitch and pull over the working thread first at D and then at E (1).

Next, the Cretan stitches are paired (2) — two close together, a space, then two more. Work the stitches as before but pair them as shown or try groups of three or four together, with a wider space between groups.

For a twisted version (3), make single, spaced Cretan stitches, wrapping each one with an extra stitch before going on to the next (E).

To end a series of stitches, thread the needle through the folded edge, between the two layers of hem, and out through the backing. Weave the loose ends into the wrong side of either the fabric or the existing stitches after the backing is removed.

Plaited Insertion

An elaborate version of the Cretan insertion, this is not difficult but takes a great deal of concentration. The secret lies in the sequence of the stitches. Follow the diagram carefully, and the result will be an exquisite stitch, well worth the effort (fig. 2-60).

With ½ to ¾ inch of backing between, baste the spaced, finished edges of two fabric pieces to a stiff-paper or cloth backing. Knot the end of thread and come up into the fold at A (1). Insert the needle from above through both layers of the hem, but not into the backing, at B (1). Pull through and down over the working thread to make the first Cretan stitch. Take a similar stitch on the lower edge at C (1), but slide the needle behind the line A B rather than over the working thread. Now, take another stitch in the upper edge to the left of B at D (2). Move back to the lower edge and work a Cretan stitch to the left of C at E (3). With the tip of the needle, weave toward F (4), over E, under the back of C, and over the top of C. Work a stitch in the upper edge at F, weaving down through the lower stitches to G (5). With a stitch in the lower edge at G, the third in the group, the lower series is finished. Weave back up to H, to the left of F (7), and work another stitch. Then weave toward I at the lower edge.

After taking a stitch at I, begin again (2), continuing the pattern of groups of three Cretan stitches joined by weaving (8:J through O). End at O by threading the needle into the fold and between the two fabric layers of the hem. After the backing has been removed, pick up the loose end and anchor it with a few tiny stitches on the wrong side of the work.

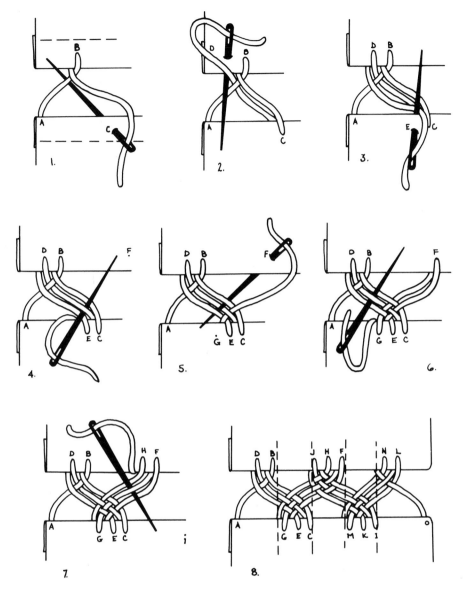

Figure 2-60. Plaited insertion.

Laced Insertion

The edging stitches described in the previous section — Antwerp edging and braid-edging stitch particularly — can be considered not only as edging or trimming stitches but as the basis for an insertion or joining. The laced insertion (fig. 2-61, 1) consists of two staggered edges of braid-edging stitch (see fig. 2-48).

Again, the two sides must be securely basted to another piece of fabric or stiff paper to ensure an even space between. With a knot at the end of a new thread, come up at E, in the fold of the hem. Overcast or lace the thread through the loops of the braid edging, ending at F on the opposite edge. Secure the thread on the wrong side of the work, with several small stitches, after the insertion is complete and the backing removed.

Variation. Try an entirely different effect with lacing. Place two rows of Antwerp edging with the loops of one row opposite the loops of the other (fig. 2-61, 2). Bind each pair of loops together with a second thread, in groups of three stitches (E to F). Start and end the threads as for regular laced insertion.

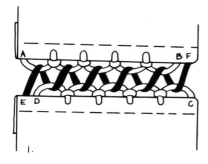

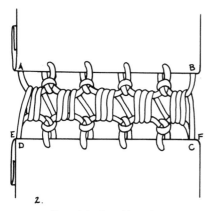

Figure 2-61. Laced insertion.

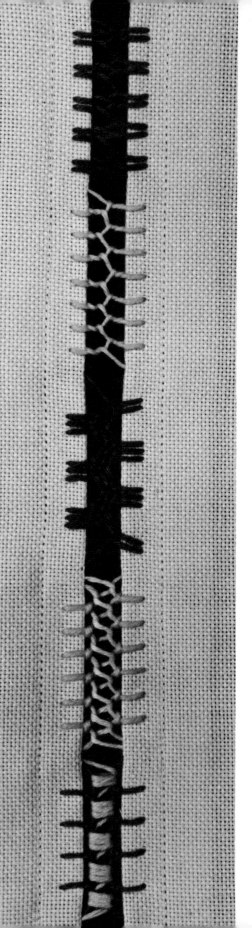

Figure 2-62, Sampler of insertion stitches. *From top to bottom*: Cretan-stitch insertion (paired), Cretan-stitch insertion (twisted), plaited insertion, laced insertion, laced-insertion variation.

Stitches on Laid or Drawn Threads

LOOPED-FILLING STITCHES

Stemstitch Band

The stemstitch, one of the basic stitches of beginning embroidery, takes on a new look when used as a detached stitch. Instead of working it directly on the background fabric, you are going to use it on a series of long straight stitches, on an area of drawn threads, or on an open warp stretched on a frame. A single row can make a segmented line; several rows, a delicate open mesh. You can work all the rows in the same direction (fig. 2-63, 3) or, for a different look, work them back and forth (4).

To practice the technique, begin at A (1), laying a series of long straight stitches in the direction of the arrows to B (1). Finish off the thread at the back of the work, and then with a new thread come up at C (1) to begin the stemstitch. Holding the working thread above the work, slide the

needle under the first vertical thread from right to left, taking care not to pick up any background fabric. Pull through, gently, to the left. Repeat the stemstitch over each vertical thread (2), working your way across to D (3) at the right-hand border.

At this point the working thread either may be carried across the back of the work to E (3) to begin the next line or, to conserve thread, brought up at F. After coming up at F, turn the entire work upside down and continue the stemstitches (2) to E (3).

Variation. Instead of repeating the line CD from F to E, try making the stitches back-to-back (4). A large area of this variation looks like very loose knitting.

There is no rule to say the stemstitch band must be worked in straight or evenly spaced lines. Try it in unevenly spaced lines, over base stitches worked in a partial circle (5).

Chevron Stemstitch

The basic stemstitch band described above is worked horizontally back and forth on vertical base stitches, while chevron stemstitch is worked in zig-zags on horizontal base stitches. It is wise to practice the former before trying the latter.

To make a sample of the chevron stemstitch, first lay a series of long straight stitches on the background fabric. Begin at A (fig. 2-65, 1), following the direction of the arrows to B (1). The sample (fig. 2-66) is on basket-weave monkscloth, and each line of stitches is 2¼ inches long, with three threads between lines.

Tack down the top and bottom lines or bars with a few small stitches (1), to keep them from pulling out of shape while you work the stemstitches. These tacks may be removed after you press the finished sample.

Now, imagine the shape of the letter M. The stemstitches will take on this shape as they are worked over the horizontal bars. Begin the filling

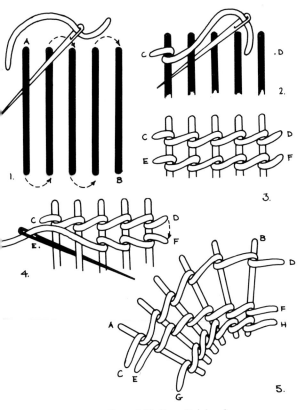

Figure 2-63. Stemstitch band.

Figure 2-64. Areas of stemstitch band are used as a filling, in this composition in cotton threads with padded suede appliqué, by the author.

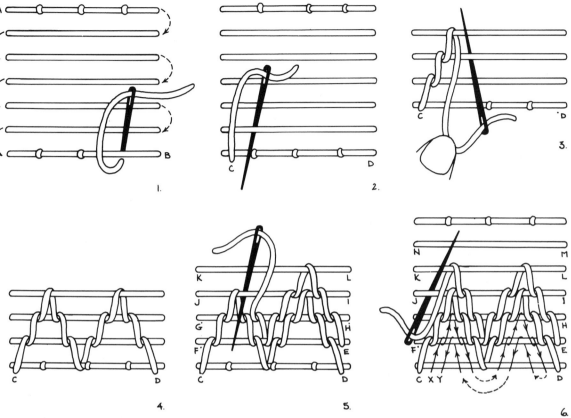

Figure 2-65. Chevron stemstitch.

with a new thread, just below the lower left corner at C (2).

Keeping the working thread to the left of the needle, work the first leg of the M by sliding the needle, from above, behind each horizontal bar. If the position of the stemstitches needs to be adjusted as you go along, this may be easily done with the point of the needle. It may help to lay your hoop or frame flat on the table to work, so you have both hands free — one to keep tension on the working thread, the other to hold the needle.

For the second leg of the M, reverse directions and work back to the bottom bar. Slide the needle behind each bar, from below this time, still keeping the working thread to the left of the needle (3). The third and fourth legs are a repeat of the first and second. End at D (4). Bring the needle up again at E (5) to start the second row. Working back to the left-hand border, make stemstitches, close to the first row, over each bar. Keep the working thread to the right of the needle all the way. At the highest point of the

design, include one more bar (5). End the return row at F (6).

After two rows you may want to change to a contrasting thread to make a bold zig-zag pattern. Repeat the first and second rows until the horizontal lines are covered. If you wish, fill in the top and bottom (6:X to Y), going through to the background fabric at the end of the rows instead of hooking over the lower bar.

Variation. Try a chevron-stemstitch border with irregular zig-zags, some high, some low, on long horizontal bars.

Figure 2-66. Sample of chevron stemstitch in two colors.

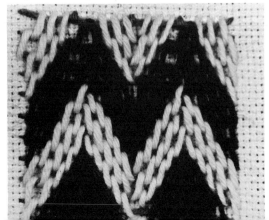

Opposite
Above: *Scarlet Web*, an exercise in raised-stem spiderweb stitch on random warp threads, by the author. Below: *Grove*, needleweaving with suede, in Swedish wool yarns on a camel-hair backing, by the author. Photo by Flo Wilson.

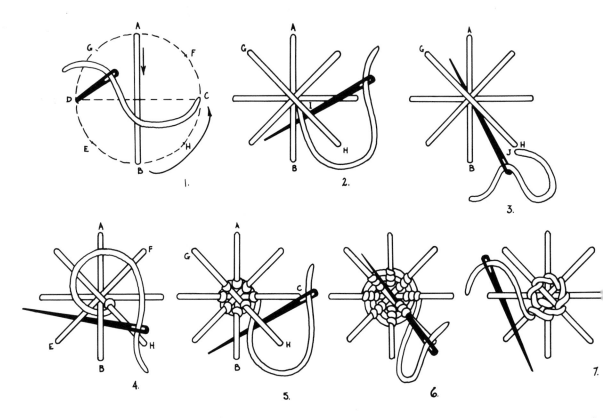

Figure 2-67. Raised-stem spiderweb stitch.

Raised-Stem Spiderweb Stitch

The raised-stem spiderweb stitch is a detached circular pattern of backstitch or stemstitch, worked on a base of long, straight, crossing stitches.

To make a sample, outline a circle, not more than 1½ inches in diameter, on the fabric. If a compass is not available, use a jar lid or coin as a guide. Knot the end of a thread, approximately 40 inches long, and come up at the top of the circle at A (fig. 2-67, 1). Make a long straight stitch by going down to the back of the work at B. Come up again at C, and work another straight stitch to D. Divide each quarter circle in half by working similar stitches from E to F and from G to H.

Without changing the thread, stitch from H across the back of the work to I (2). Bring the needle up through the fabric under the point where the straight stitches cross, then out to the front between B and H. If you want the web to be completely detached in the center, come up at J (3), as close to H as possible. Slide the needle under the crossed straight stitches and up between A and G, taking care not to pick up any background fabric. The extra thread from J will be

incorporated with the line G H in the working of the top stitches.

Begin the looped filling, in a clockwise direction, by sliding the needle from right to left under the line G H and under the line A B (2). Pull through, keeping tension on the working thread, while pushing the loop toward the center with the needle's tip. Make the next stitch by again sliding the needle from right to left, this time under the line A B and the line E F (4). Continue these stitches in a clockwise direction, each time taking the needle back over one and under two base threads (5). Cover the base threads completely with stitches, or leave them partly exposed. To finish off a thread, slide the needle toward the center through the core of the ribbed stitches, and snip the end off flush (6). To start a new thread, reverse this step.

You can change the look of this finished stitch by working the filling clockwise over two and under one base thread (7).

Variation. Using a 4-inch embroidery hoop, stitch a random crisscross warp. Where the most threads cross, work raised-stem spiderwebs in various sizes and colors (fig. 2-69).

Figure 2-68. A repeat pattern of raised stem spiderwebs alternates with needleweaving motifs on gingham check fabric. Courtesy of Beverly Rush.

Figure 2-69. Raised stem spiderwebs in varied sizes and colors on a ramdom warp, which was stretched between the edges of a 4-inch circle.

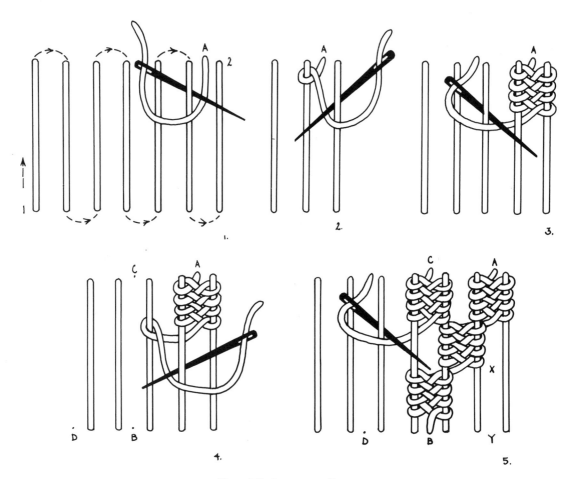

Figure 2-70. Cretan open filling.

Cretan Open Filling

To learn the Cretan open filling (fig. 2-70), work a base on the background fabric of a series of straight stitches or bars that are 2 inches long and ½ inch apart.

Using a yarn of knitting worsted or substitute of same weight, start stitching into the background in the lower left, in the direction of the arrows, and finish the thread off at the upper right at the back of the fabric (1:1 to 2).

Prepare a new thread, approximately 36 inches long, which is enough to complete one phase of the filling. Use a blunt tapestry needle to keep from splitting the threads. Bring the needle and thread up at A (1). Begin the filling by sliding the needle from left to right under the second bar and over the working thread. Change to the right-hand bar, and again slide the needle under it and over the working thread, this time from right to left (2).

Continue alternating these stitches four times on each side, taking care not to pick up the background fabric but only the long straight stitches.

To change from one pair of bars to the next, take the working thread to the left under the second bar and over the third. Slide the needle under the third bar, from left to right, and over the working thread to begin the second group (3).

Keeping an even tension, repeat the groups of filling stitches three times, changing to another pair of bars after each group.

Finish off the thread at the back of the work at B (5).

With a new thread, start the previous procedure again at C, ending at D (5). Continue the stair-step groups, until the whole space is filled in a checkerboard pattern. To complete the lower right-hand corner, thread the needle down through the finished Cretan open-filling stitches and out at X (5). Work a single group of stitches to Y.

Variation. Using different weights of yarn, stitch freely within the designated space, alternating the Cretan open-filling stitch with corded bars (see fig. 2-119).

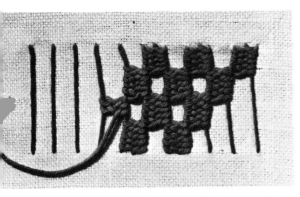

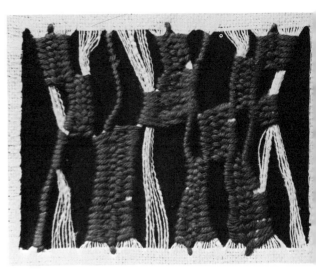

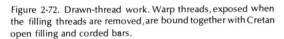

Figure 2-71.Cretan open filling forms a traditional checkerboard pattern on a base of evenly spaced laid threads.

Figure 2-72. Drawn-thread work. Warp threads, exposed when the filling threads are removed, are bound together with Cretan open filling and corded bars.

Figure 2-73. Cut-through appliqué in wavy lines is accentuated by vertical rows of detached Cretan stitch in two weights of thread.

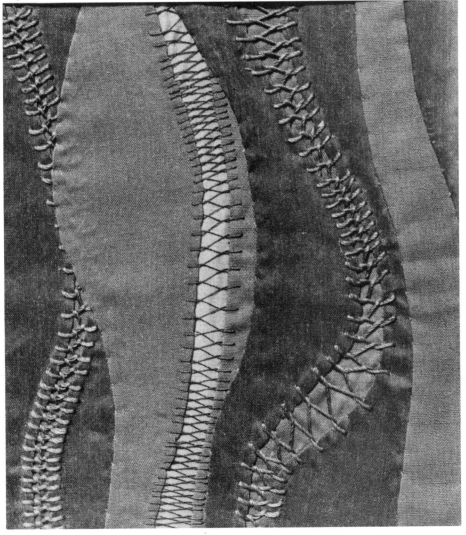

Russian-Overcast Filling

This filling was traditionally worked on a base of drawn threads, those left behind when some warp and some filling threads are pulled out of the background fabric. It works equally well, however, on a grid made of vertical and horizontal long straight stitches.

Beginning with the verticals, come up at A (fig. 2-74, 1). Work in the direction of the arrows, spacing the bars evenly as you go. End at the back of the work at H.

Next, lay the horizontal bars. With a new thread, come up at I (1) and again work evenly spaced stitches in the direction of the arrows. End at P.

When the base threads are complete, tie them together with overcasting stitches worked in a stair-step pattern. Begin just below P (2). Slide the needle, from above, behind the horizontal thread, and pull through snugly. Repeat, to make two overcasting stitches.

Where P and B intersect, change directions by sliding the needle behind the vertical thread, from right to left (3). Pull through, making a long overcasting stitch across the intersection. Work one more stitch around the vertical thread. End by going down into the background fabric to the right of B.

With a new thread, begin the overcasting again just below M (4). Work the same as for lines P and B (3). Where they intersect, cross over to the horizontal by sliding the needle, from above, behind the horizontal thread (4). Continue to C, overcasting in this stair-step pattern — first make the "tread" of the stair and then the "riser". Repeat from L to F, and from I to G (5). At the bottom of the design, where the verticals must be worked first, begin to the left of A (5). Continue the filling until all the base threads are overcast.

Increase the number of overcasting stitches per square to suit the thickness of yarn and the space between base threads. For a heavier look and more prominent ridges, try another layer of overcasting, perhaps in a different color.

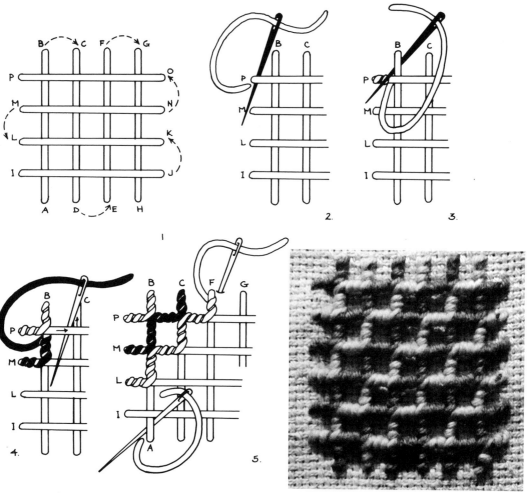

Figure 2-74. Russian-overcast filling.

Figure 2-75. Sample of Russian-overcast filling in two colors.

Raised Honeycomb Filling

Raised honeycomb filling is an entirely different stitch from the basic honeycomb filling (see fig. 2-85). The raised filling is worked on vertical and horizontal bars rather than woven on diagonals. To create a heavily textured dimensional effect, layers of overcasting are worked over a base of laid threads.

Use a hoop or frame to keep the background fabric taut. Work a grid of evenly spaced straight stitches, starting the vertical threads at A (fig. 2-76, 1) and ending at B. Begin the horizontal stitches at C, working over the first layer in the direction of the arrows to D (1).

With a new thread, bring the needle up again at A (2) to start the overcasting. Wrap each vertical thread binding in the horizontals as you work (3), and be sure not to pick up any of the background fabric. When the verticals are completed, overcast each horizontal thread from left to right, starting at C (4).

Vary the number of overcasting stitches per line to experiment with texture. Stitches far apart make the work smoother; stitches close together create a lumpier and heavier look.

At this stage, the filling may be left as is or embellished with another series of overcasting stitches. A change of thread color will also add textural interest. Start again at A (5), and follow the shaded line in the diagram. Holding the work so the verticals are in a horizontal position, work a long overcasting stitch, over the base threads, in each space of the grid. At the end of the line return to A working in the opposite direction, thus making a cross at each intersection (6). When the vertical threads are all bound, start at C and complete the horizontals in one of two ways. Either repeat as for the verticals, making a heavy, raised star effect (7, Row 1) or slide the needle behind each intersection, forming a separate cross in each space (7, Row 3). Secure any loose ends of thread by weaving them into the wrong side of the border stitches.

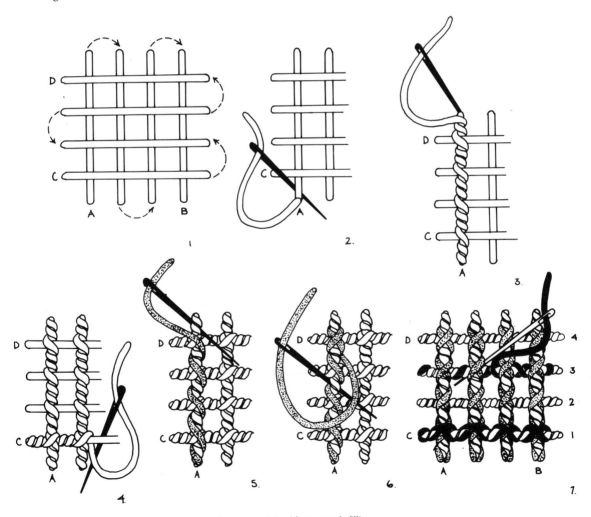

Figure 2-76. Raised honeycomb filling.

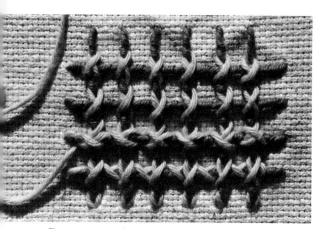

Figure 2-77. Sample of raised honeycomb filling in two colors.

Knotted Grid for Filling Stitches

Filet stitch (see fig. 2-43) is worked diagonally with a single thread that is knotted at each intersection. When done properly, which requires some patience, the result is a vertical and horizontal grid pattern, useful as a base for looped or woven filling stitches. Working the grid can be tedious if you are anxious to experiment with the overstitching, so, as a result, I have devised a method of stitching a quick and easy grid (fig. 2-78).

With a knot at the end of the thread, come up at A (1) and work horizontal long stitches on the background fabric in the direction of the arrows to F.

To begin the verticals, come up at G (2). Hold the working thread taut over the line A B with the left thumb. Work a coral knot (see fig. 1-35) by sliding the needle from the upper left behind the intersection of both threads and out over the working thread (2). Keep the thumb in place as long as possible while tightening the knot. Work similar knots over the lines D C and E F, going down into the background at H (3). Beginning each time at the top of the work, complete the knotted verticals from I to J, K to L and M to N. Finish off the thread at the back of the work.

Ghost-stitch filling. Ghost stitch is only one of the many looped filling stitches traditionally worked into areas of filet lace. It can also be worked into the knotted grid. It is made in rows with a single detached buttonhole stitch with one right-side-up row followed by one upside-down row.

Begin the stitching at O (4), and use a contrasting thread to see the stitches more easily. Work a loose buttonhole stitch over the horizontal line between each vertical, letting the loops fall just below the halfway mark of each small square. Go down into the background at P, then come up, slightly above, at Q.

Now, turn the work upside down (5). Repeat the buttonhole stitches as for the first row, but between each stitch weave the needle over the loop of the previous row, behind the vertical, and out again over the loop. Go down at R.

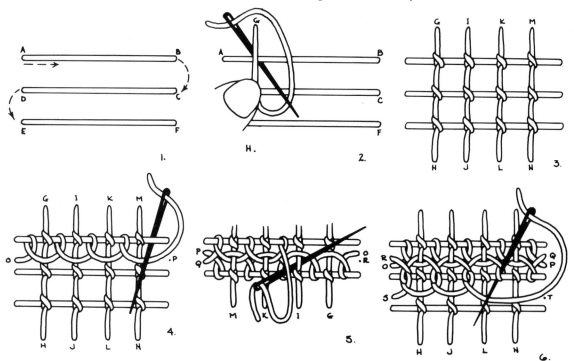

Figure 2-78. Knotted grid for filling stitches.

Turn the work right side up again. Beginning at S (6) work the third row as the first, but this time thread the top of each loop through the eye of the loop in the second row. Go down into the fabric at T. The fourth row is a repeat of the second.

Variation. Try making an open and closed pattern on the same base grid, by filling in alternate squares with plain over-and-under weaving.

Figure 2-79. Sample, of knotted grid for filling stitches, with looped top-stitching of ghost stitch.

Figure 2-80. *Cream on Cream*, by Fritzi Oxley. Threads withdrawn from the cotton homespun backing are used to work looped ghost stitch over the remaining threads.

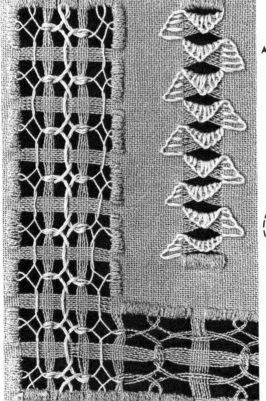

WOVEN-FILLING STITCHES

Surface Darning

Surface darning is a detached embroidery stitch, worked on a fabric background, using basic weaving techniques to fill any shaped area.

For a rectangle in plain weave — over one, under one — knot the end of the thread, and come up at A (fig. 2-81, 1). Work a series of horizontal straight stitches, evenly spaced on the background fabric, following the direction of the arrows to B (1). In the diagram, these straight threads are widely spaced to show the structure of the stitch more clearly. Try a sample this way first, and then experiment with narrower or wider spaces between or with thicker or thinner yarn.

With the same thread or a new contrasting thread, come up from the back at C (2) to begin the vertical filling. Weave with the needle from top to bottom toward D, alternating under, then over. Go down into the cloth at D, then up again at E, to begin the second vertical.

Work toward F, at the top of the work, weaving over the horizontals where the line C D goes under and under where C D goes over. Go down at F, then up again at G, to begin the third vertical, which is a repeat of C D.

Continue the vertical filling to the right edge of the work, alternating C D and E F. Go down to the back of the work at P, finishing off the thread with several small stitches into the fabric.

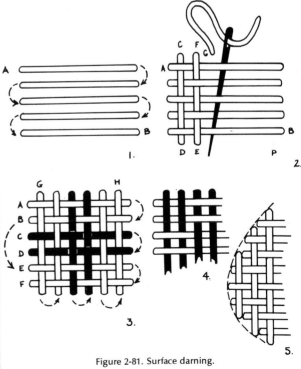

Figure 2-81. Surface darning.

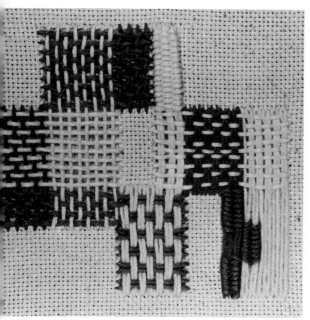

Figure 2-82. Sampler of surface darning, using combinations of single and paired threads.

Variation. For an area of plaid, begin the horizontals in the same way, but alternate equal numbers of threads in two different colors to make a series of stripes (3). Keep two needles threaded, one in each color. Work straight stitches in the first color from A to B. Go down to the back of the work, and leave the needle and thread dangling. Begin the second color at C, and work straight stitches to D. Let this thread dangle from the back, and pick up the first color again to continue from E to F. Keeping the first color in hand, make a stitch across the back of the work to G to begin the darning as before (2). Alternate the vertical stripes like the horizontals, ending at the top right side at H (3).

Try a basket-weave pattern by alternating two threads over and under in both directions (4), or fill a curved shape with surface darning (5).

Woven Band or Filling

Woven band is a richly patterned filling stitch, woven on a base of horizontal threads, that uses two separate needles threaded with contrasting yarns. For making this stitch, several books in the past have described a laborious method of picking up and putting down the two needles each time a stitch is taken. Figure 2-83 shows a much quicker and easier way to achieve the same intricate result.

To make a sample, knot the end of a length of yarn and come up at A (1). Work a series of evenly spaced, ladder-like straight stitches in the direc-

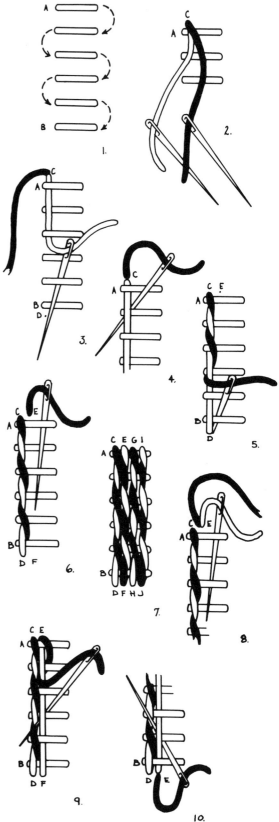

Figure 2-83. Woven band.

tion of the arrows to B. This base will be completely covered by the weaving, so the choice of yarn color is not too important. After learning the stitch, try extending the base threads to make a square rather than a band.

Cut two contrasting threads to an equal length, then thread each one on a separate needle and knot the two ends together. Thread one needle at a time through the same hole to the front of the work at C (2).

To start the weaving, always remember to go under the top rung of the ladder first, regardless of which color you are using. Let the dark thread dangle, then with the light thread weave under and over the rungs toward D (3). Take the light thread to the back of the work at D and let it dangle. Now, pick up the dark thread. Take a stitch diagonally, from the upper right to the lower left, behind both threads at each point where C D crosses over a horizontal (4). Go down at D (5).

For a diagonal pattern (7), keep the dark thread in hand, taking a long stitch across the back of the work to E (6). Weave to F (6), as you did toward D. Now, bring the light thread through at E, taking stitches around the dark thread as before (4 and 5). Work G to H (7) like C D, and I to J like E F. Finish off the band by taking the two contrasting threads through the same hole to the back of the work at J (7). Tie the two ends together against the fabric, in a square knot. Clip off the excess thread.

To make a striped band, begin each time by

Figure 2-84. Sampler of woven band stitches. *From left to right:* diagonal, striped, tweedy, and zig-zag woven band. *Below:* striped band on base stitches arranged in a curved line.

going under the top rung with the light thread (8 and 9).

For a tweedy look or a bold zig-zag (fig. 2-84), use the same technique as for the diagonal or the stripe, but stitch in both directions rather than only from top to bottom (10). The woven surface stitches will follow any arrangement of base threads; try it in a curve or a circle (fig. 2-84).

Honeycomb Filling

Honeycomb filling is a series of interwoven straight stitches crossing at angles. The finished pattern resembles caning. Although it looks complicated, it is quite simple to work (fig. 2-85).

To learn the honeycomb filling, use a 4-inch embroidery hoop and three separate colors of knitting worsted on a background of basket-weave monkscloth. The hoop makes its own border, eliminating the need to draw a circle on the fabric. The circular shape makes the actual working of the stitch easier, as you are not concerned with ends of lines meeting perfectly, but rather with the spacing between the lines. The contrasting yarns make it much easier to see the construction of each layer.

Starting with one color, work a set of horizontal lines ½ inch apart (1: 1 to 2). Then, with a second color, shaded in Diagram 2, bring the needle and thread up at 3. Lay a series of threads, ½ inch apart, diagonally over the first ones. With the third color, come up at A (2). Weave toward B diagonally with the needle, at right angles to the second color. Alternately pass over the diagonal thread and pick up the lower horizontal thread at each point where the first two colors cross. Go down to the back of the work at B, coming up again at C to begin the next line of weaving to D. Repeat from C to D, and continue the third layer in this way until the circle is filled.

Remove the hoop and weave in any loose ends of thread on the wrong side of the work.

Variation. Try another sample using a finer thread, or a heavier thread, perhaps in a square or rectangle. This time place the threads closer together for a very rich woven texture.

For honeycomb filling in a square or rectangle, a little planning is necessary to make the pattern work out correctly. To learn the technique, use a background of needlepoint canvas (10 or 12 holes to the inch) or a loosely woven fabric, because the stitch works best when the spaces or threads are large and easily counted.

Lay the horizontal threads first. Begin at A (fig. 2-85a, 1), and work an evenly spaced series of long straight stitches in the direction of the ar-

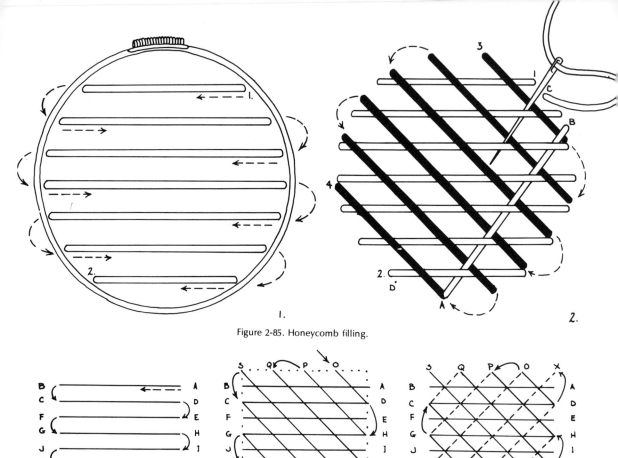

Figure 2-85. Honeycomb filling.

Figure 2-85a. Honeycomb filling in a square or rectangle.

rows to N. The space between A and D must divide evenly into the length of A B, so that the shapes formed by the intersection of the diagonals are squares. For the sample, using the threads in the background fabric as a guide, count two threads between A and D, and 16 threads for the length of A B. Later, experiment with other combinations. For example, lines four threads apart may be 32 threads long, or six apart, 24 long.

The second step, more easily seen if worked in a different color, is to lay a series of diagonals over the horizontals. Begin at O (2), located by counting up from A two threads, then to the left four threads. Make a straight stitch to D, then come up again at H. Pass over the horizontals to P (four threads to the left of O). Keeping the same spacing, work long stitches in the direction of the arrows, ending at the back of the work at V (2).

In a third color begin the final step at T (3). Weave to L, under the horizontal M N and over the diagonal S R. Come up at H, weave to U, by

Figure 2-86. Patchwork sampler of honeycomb filling in rectangular shapes.

84

going under the horizontal thread and over the diagonal thread at each intersection. Repeat this pattern of weaving to complete the filling, and end at Q (3).

A patchwork of variously shaped rectangles in honeycomb filling could make a handsome quilt top (fig. 2-86).

Figure 2-87. Small quilt with patches of honeycomb filling in cotton rug yarn, by Judy Kasperson.

Figure 2-88. Basket with areas of woven caning that resemble honeycomb filling embroidery stitch. Courtesy of Jacqueline Enthoven.

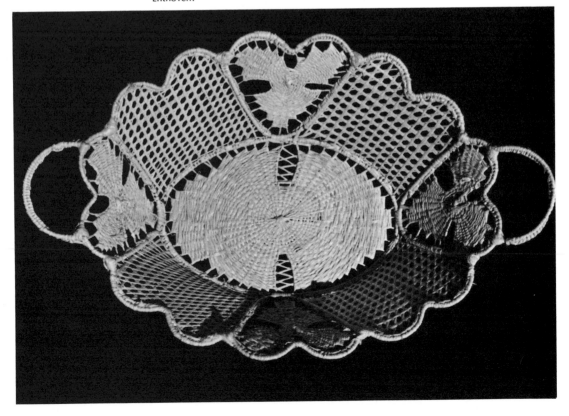

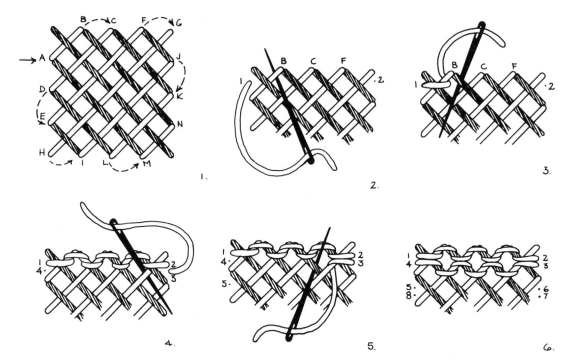

Figure 2-89. Twisted lattice filling.

Twisted Lattice Filling

Twisted lattice filling resembles a textured, open grillwork. A base of diagonal straight stitches, woven together with similar or contrasting yarns, is then laced with a third yarn for an intricate twisting effect.

Using knitting worsted or substitute of equal weight, begin the base by bringing the needle and thread up at A (fig. 2-89, 1). To locate B, count threads in the background fabric so that there are as many threads between B and the top left corner as between A and the top left corner.

Try using a 2-over-2 monkscloth, with an eight-thread space. Go down into the fabric at B. Come up at C, eight spaces from B. Cross over and go down at D, eight spaces from A. Come up again at E, and continue this pattern of diagonals to N (1). Finish the thread off in the back of the work at N.

With a new length of the same yarn or another color, start the opposite diagonals by coming up in the same hole as I (1). Go down at E. Come up again at D, weave first over E F, then under G H, then over I J. Go down at L. Come up at M and continue the diagonals, weaving over and then under each time. End the series at F (1).

With another new length of yarn, begin at I (2). Slide the needle, from below, behind the base thread to the left of B. Pull the thread through, keeping it fairly taut. Then, slide the needle, from above this time, behind the next base thread, to the right of B (3). Repeat these two steps, ending

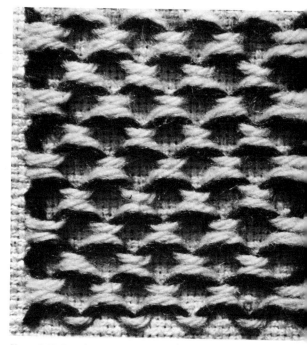

Figure 2-90. Sample of twisted lattice filling in two colors.

at 2. Bring the needle up again at 3, and work the lacing in the opposite direction as shown in Diagram 4. Slide the needle first from above (4) and then from below (5). End this row at 4.

Repeat the first and second rows, and watch the pattern develop.

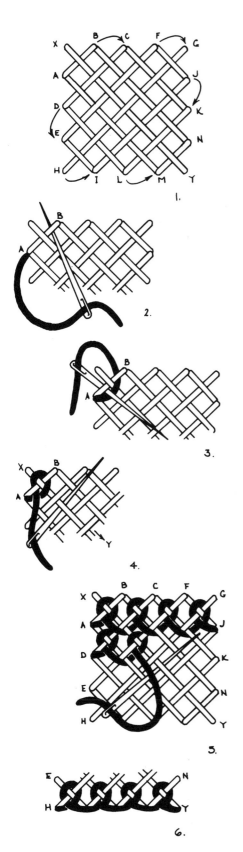

Figure 2-91. Laced lattice filling.

Figure 2-92. Sample of laced lattice filling, in contrasting colors.

Laced Lattice Filling

While experimenting with the interlacing stitches described in the next section, I became excited about trying looped stitches over the woven base used for twisted lattice. The result is an exquisite, textured filling, which I have called laced lattice (fig. 2-91).

Lay the diagonal base threads (1) by following the instructions for twisted lattice. With the base complete, knot the end of a second contrasting thread, and come up at A (2) to begin the looped stitching. To make the work easier, think of each set of crossing threads as a separate unit around which a circle is woven in a counter-clockwise direction. To weave the circle, slide the needle from the lower right under the line A B, just below B (2). Then, slide the needle from the upper left, under the line A B, which is just above A (3), and over the working thread. To secure the base of the loop, slide the needle under X Y (4). Repeat (2, 3, 4) to the end of the row, going down into the fabric at J (5). Take a long stitch from right to left across the back of the work and come up at D to begin the second row, from D to K (5). Work a third row from E to N (5). On the last row, H to Y (6), omit sliding the needle under X Y (4).

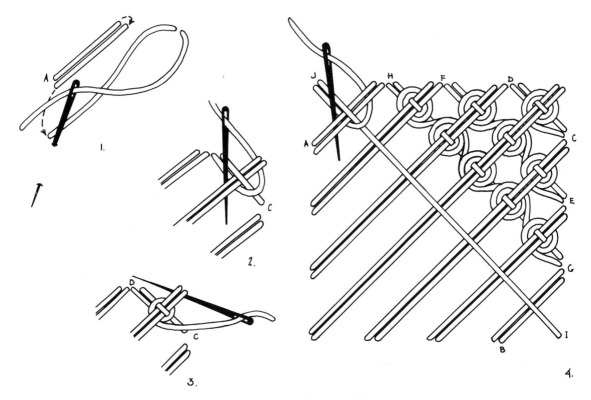

Figure 2-93. Double bars with woven-circle filling.

Double Bars with Woven-Circle Filling

To make this delicate pattern of circles or wheels over a lattice-like background, knot the end of the thread and bring the needle up at A (fig. 2-93, 1). Working in the direction of the arrows and catching the background fabric at both ends, lay a series of diagonal double threads in the shape of a square. End the thread at the back of the work at B (4).

With a new thread, bring the needle up at C (2). Lay the working thread at right angles over the base threads, and catch the background fabric at D. Return the working thread to C by weaving counterclockwise under the base threads, over the stitch just made, then under the base threads again (2). Repeat this step as many times as you wish for a wider circle (3). Bring the needle and thread to the back of the work just below C.

For the next row, come up at E (4). Again lay the working thread at right angles across the base threads, and catch the background fabric at F. Return the working thread to E by alternating the weaving of the wheels, first counterclockwise, then clockwise. This makes the intricate spiral pattern.

Repeat this process from G to H and I to J, continuing until the whole area is filled. Increase or decrease the number of wheels as necessary in each row to complete the pattern.

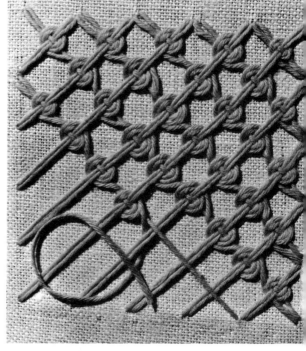

Figure 2-94. Sample of double bars with woven-circle filling on linen.

BORDERS AND INTERLACING STITCHES

Raised Chain Band

Raised chain band is a versatile, textured stitch, useful for single lines or as a filling, and equally suitable for dramatic borders in straight lines or abstract areas in curved lines (fig. 2-95).

The stitch is worked in two stages. First the ladder-like base of laid threads is made and then the raised chain over these threads. Only at the beginning and end of the chain row does the needle enter the background fabric. A random arrangement of long straight stitches (6) may be substituted for the traditional ladder base. The chain also may be worked over sections of other completed stitches (fig. 2-96).

For a sample, make a ladder base by bringing the needle and thread up at A (1). Follow the direction of the arrows, making short stitches on the background fabric, to B (1). Finish off the thread at the back of the work.

With a new thread, possibly of a contrasting color, come up in the center at C (2), above the top rung. Slide the needle, from below, under the top rung. Pull through and up to the left. Then, holding the working thread down with your left thumb, slide the needle, from above this time, under the top rung and over the working thread (3). This completes the chain. Move to the next rung, still holding the working thread down to keep the tension even, and repeat (4), as in steps 2 and 3.

If you run out of thread during the chaining process, tack down the loop of the chain at D (5). Then, with a new thread, come up again above the loop and continue on. The new thread will hide the end of the old.

Variation. Place a series of long straight stitches at random on the background fabric. Work rows of chain over them, close together, as a filling (6). Or, try the chain over warp threads in a background material where the filling has been removed.

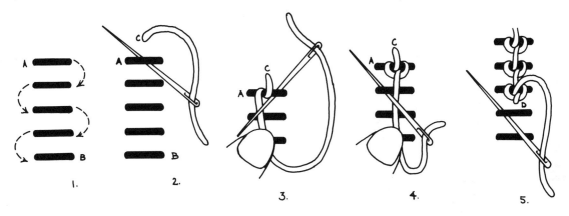

1. 2. 3. 4. 5.

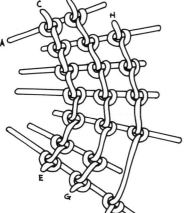

6.

Figure 2-95 Raised chain band.

Figure 2-96. Detail of a textured hanging, by the author, on knitted background fabric. Three rows of raised chain band form a vertical stripe over long straight stitches, and, to the left, stemstitch band is used as a filling.

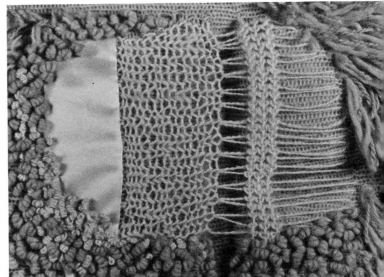

Checkered Chain Band

Checkered chain band is made like raised chain band, on a ladder base of straight stitches. To learn the stitch, use a narrow base in a vertical line, with a single row of chain. (fig. 2-97). Later, vary the base stitches by making them narrow or wide, in straight or curved lines, or holding a single row or many rows of chain. The finished band looks best when the base threads are evenly spaced and close together.

over the base stitches (4:F, G, H). Go down at I, which is centered below the bottom rung.

Take a long stitch across the back of the work to E, or start a new thread. Finish the chain with the light-color thread, and again slide the needle behind the points where the dark thread crosses over the base stitches, only on the right side of the work this time (5). Go down to the back of the work at I, and finish off the thread.

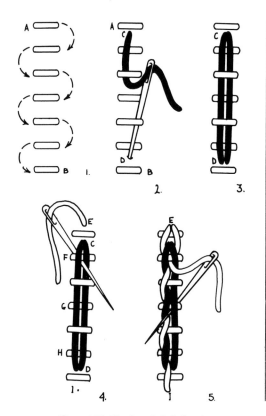

Figure 2-97. Checkered chain band.

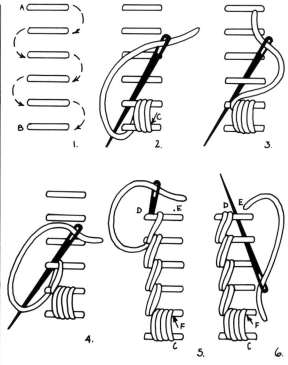

Figure 2-98. Portuguese border.

Portuguese Border

Knot the end of the thread and come up at A (1). Work a ladder with an uneven number of rungs by taking small stitches into the background fabric in the direction of the arrows to B (1).

For the top chain, choose two contrasting colors of the same weight of yarn. Start with the darker color, coming up at C (2) between the two top rungs of the ladder. Weave first over and then under each rung to D, which is between the two bottom rungs of the ladder. Come up again to the right of D and repeat the weaving to C, making a double thread (3).

Now, with the light color yarn, come up at E, centered above the top rung. Slide the needle from above, diagonally behind both threads, at every point where the left dark thread crosses

Portuguese border is a narrow band of stem-stitches (see fig. 2-63), worked in both directions on a ladder base of straight stitches. The sample (left, fig. 2-99) is made with D.M.C. Retors à Broder Cotton, with the rungs of the ladder ½ inch long and ¼ inch apart.

For your sample, work a similar ladder base, using any number of stitches (fig. 2-98, 1:A to B). Begin the top stitching at the base of the ladder by making a series of four satin stitches as a spacer for the stemstitches. To do this, bring the thread up under and out below the bottom rung at C (2). Slide the needle, from above, behind the two lower rungs, and pull through to make a loose satin stitch. Work two more similar stitches. Then, on the fourth stitch, slide the needle, from above, behind the second rung only.

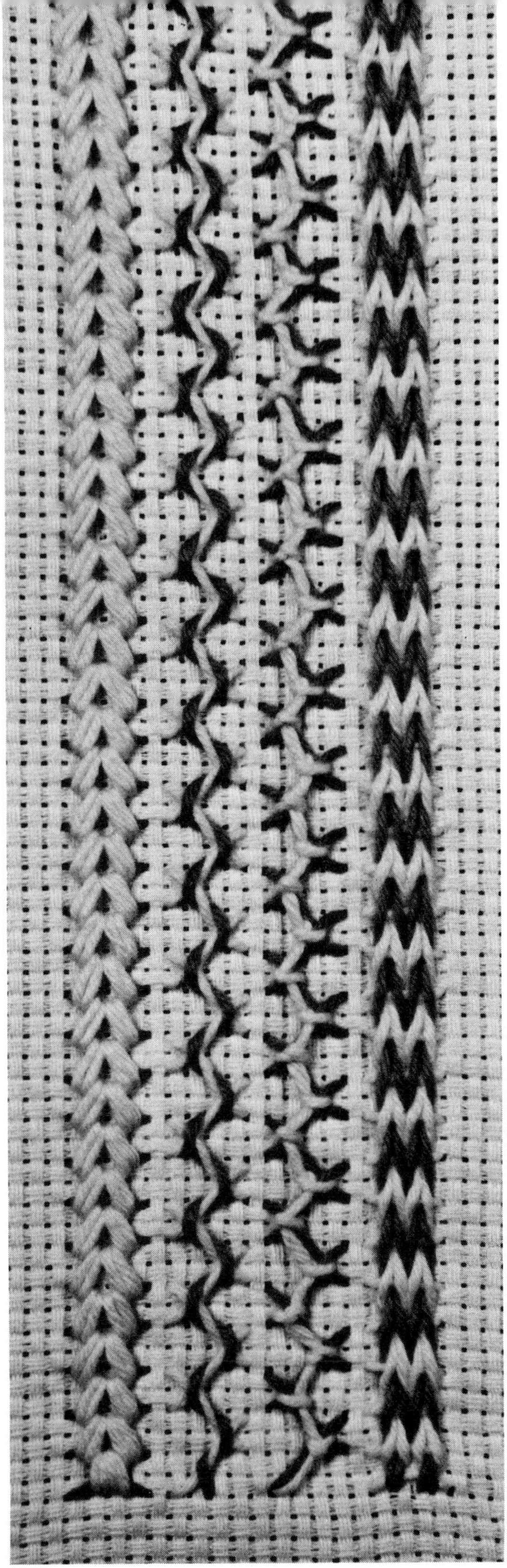

Work toward A, up the left side, making two slanting stitches over each pair of rungs. Slide the needle once behind both rungs (3), then once behind only the top rung (4).

When you reach the top rung, finish the second stitch by going down to the back of the work at D (5). Come up at E (6) to start the stitching down the right side. Again work pairs of stitches over the rungs (3, 4), but this time slide the needle from below (6). End the last pair by going down to the back of the work at F.

Band in interlacing

To learn the band in interlacing, first work two parallel rows of backstitch, about ¾ inch apart. Stagger the rows like a brick wall so the center of each lower stitch overlaps the end of each upper stitch (fig. 2-100, 1). Later, when this step becomes more familiar, try making the two lines wavy or in a circle or with wide and narrow spaces between.

With the anchoring backstitches in place, begin the filling by coming up at A (2). Working from above, slide the needle behind the first upper backstitch. With the working thread under the point of the needle, pull through and gently downward.

Now, slide the needle, from below, under the first lower backstitch. Pull through over the working thread and upward.

The combination of these two steps forms a loose, detached Cretan stitch, tying together the two rows of backstitches.

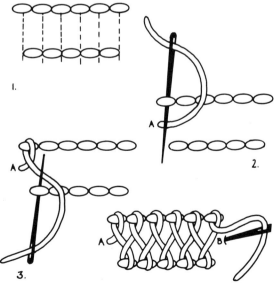

Figure 2-100. Band in interlacing.

Figure 2-99. Sample of border stitches. *From left to right:* Portuguese border, threaded herringbone stitch, tied herringbone stitch, checkered chain band.

Figure 2-101. Sample of band in interlacing in two colors.

Alternate the Cretan stitches from the upper to the lower backstitches to complete the row. End at B (4) at the back of the work.

Tied Herringbone Stitch

As you have discovered, many detached border stitches, or bands, are made on a ladder base of straight stitches. Try a change of pace with the tied herringbone (fig. 2-102) or threaded herringbone, described below. Both are made on a base of plain herringbone stitch.

Outline the width of your border by stitching two parallel rows of basting on the background fabric. Knot the end of the thread and come up at A (1) on the lower line. Take a horizontal stitch from right to left on the upper line, from B to C. Move back to the lower line and take another horizontal stitch from D to E (2). Alternate these steps to finish the base, ending at P (3).

For the top stitching, use a contrasting color thread and come up in the same hole as P (4). Tie each point where the base threads cross with a coral knot. Lay the working thread in a loose counter-clockwise loop and hold it in place with the left thumb. Slide the needle, from above, behind the crossing threads at O and N, behind the loop, and out over the base of the loop. Pull through to make the knot. Work a similar knot between M and L (5) on the lower line. Alternate these steps, working back toward A (6). Take the thread down to the back of the work in the same hole as A.

Threaded Herringbone Stitch

For a border of threaded herringbone stitch, work the base stitches as for tied herringbone.

The top stitching or threading is very similar to twisted lattice (see fig. 2-89). Choose a contrasting-color thread, and come up at X (fig. 2-103, 4). Slide the needle from below, behind the line A B (4). Then slide it from above, behind the line C D (5). Repeat these two steps to the end of the herringbone base. Finish off the thread by going down to the back of the work at Y (7), and weaving into the wrong side of the stitches.

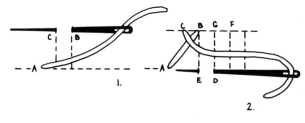

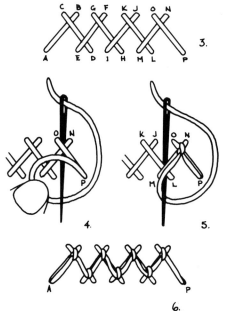

Figure 2-102. Tied herringbone stitch.

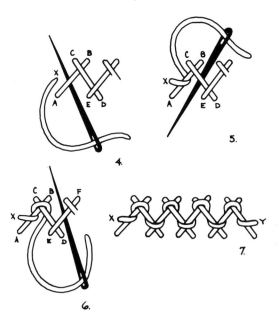

Figure 2-103. Threaded herringbone stitch.

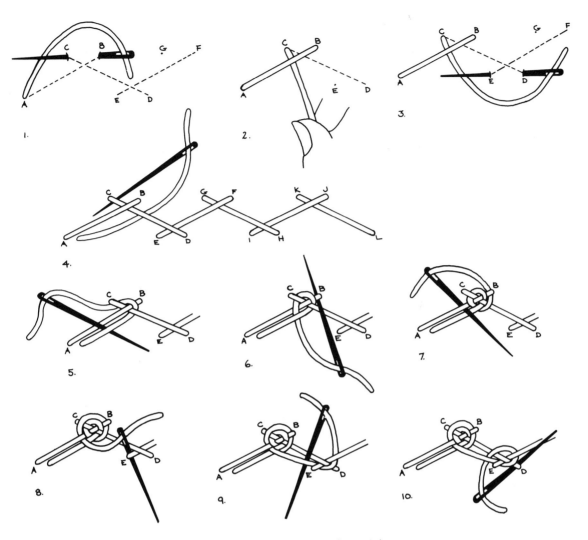

Figure 2-104. Laced herringbone stitch.

Laced Herringbone Stitch

For lacing on a base of herringbone stitch, the herringbone must be constructed differently from that in the tied and threaded versions. Come up at A (fig. 2-104, 1). Insert the needle at B, and bring it out at C. Now, with the working thread behind the point of the needle, pull through, and then downward (2). You will notice that this motion makes the line A B cross over the line C D. To continue the herringbone, insert the needle at D, and bring it out at E (3). Pull through over the working thread and up this time. Work another stitch from F to G, the same as the first from B to C. Make the herringbone base as long as you wish, in a straight line, a curved line, or perhaps a circle. To finish, take the thread to the back of the work and weave it into the wrong side of the stitches.

With a new thread in a contrasting color, begin the lacing to the right of A (4). Weave with the needle in a counter-clockwise direction, first under C D, then over A B, under C D, over A B, and under the working thread (5). Continue weaving in the same direction for a second circle, this time over C D, under A B (6), over C D, under A B, and over the working thread (7).

Figure 2-105. Sample of laced herringbone stitch in two colors.

The upper circle now complete, bring the working thread to the lower cross of the herringbone stitch. Again working in a counterclockwise direction, slide the needle under E F (8), over C D, under E F, over C D, and under the working thread (9). Slide the needle under C D (10) to finish the lacing. Continue alternating the upper and lower circles to the end of the herringbone base. Finish the interlacing to the left of L (4) by taking the thread to the back of the work.

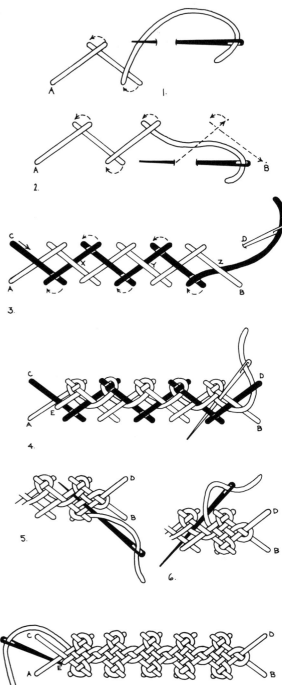

Figure 2-106. Bands of laced herringbone stitched by the author in ivory D.M.C. Perle Cotton size 3, from shoulder to hemline, on an ivory satin wedding dress. Courtesy of Mrs. Charles Hewitson and Mrs. E. L. Miller.

Interlacing Stitch on a Base of Double Herringbone

Interlacing stitch looks like a richly textured braid. It is composed of three basic steps — a row of herringbone, another row of herringbone, and the interlacing over all. To learn the stitch, it helps to use a different color yarn for each step. The trick is to work the base of herringbone correctly. Study Figure 2-107: 1,2 carefully to see

Figure 2-107. Interlacing stitch on a base of double herringbone.

how the threads cross, and then use them as a guide for your first row.

With another color yarn, begin the second row of herringbone at C (3). Work exactly like the first row, but take care to slide the needle under the existing thread at X, Y, and Z (3). End at D.

Now, you are ready for the interlacing. A good rule to remember for this stitch is that no two adjacent threads ever go over or under in the same pattern. They always alternate as in weaving. With your third color, bring the thread up at E (4). Follow Diagram 4 carefully, making loops over the top cross of each herringbone. At the end of the base stitches, reverse directions as shown. Continue back to E (4), working the loops over the bottom cross of each herringbone, and at the same time weaving into the base of the upper loops (5 and 6). End at E (7) at the back of the work.

Interlacing takes considerable concentration and patience, but the results are worth it.

Variation. Try this stitch as an insertion, a decorative means of joining two finished edges. Insertion stitches are described beginning on page 62.

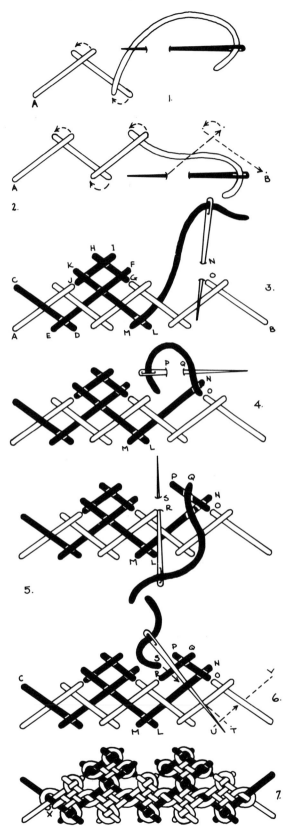

Figure 2-108. Sample of interlacing stitch on a base of double herringbone in two colors.

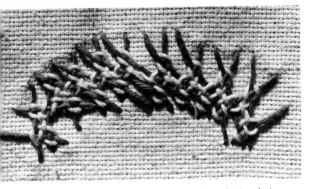

Figure 2-109. Herringbone stitches, as a base for interlacing, can be distorted or arranged in any shape.

Interlacing Stitch on Double-Herringbone Variation

After experimenting with interlacing on a base of double herringbone, I tried this elegant variation. Work the first row of herringbone as before (fig. 2-110, 1 and 2). Thread the needle with a different-color yarn, and begin the second herringbone row at C (3). The construction of this row is just like the interlacing on a base of double herringbone, except for an extra "top-knot" that extends up between each existing stitch. The "top-knot" is made by several herringbone-like

Figure 2-110. Interlacing stitch on double-herringbone variation.

stitches, worked counterclockwise (3, 4, and 5), and then down to a plain herringbone at the lower edge. Follow each step on the diagram from C through to V (6).

Before beginning the interlacing, it might be helpful to refer to Figure 2-107, which shows interlacing on a base of double herringbone. Working from left to right with one continuous thread, begin at X (7) weaving loops around each cross in the upper part of the design. At the end of the row, reverse directions, returning to X (as in fig. 2-107, 4, 5 and 6) by weaving on the lower herringbone stitches.

The combination of both interlacing techniques in a circular motif around a beach rock is shown in Figure 1-42.

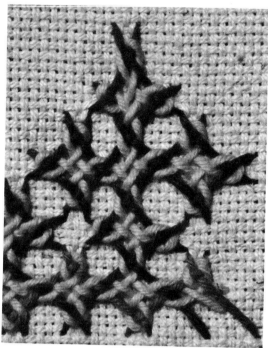

Figure 2-111. Sample of interlacing stitch on double-herringbone variation in contrasting colors.

Figure 2-112. Sample of an elaborate variation of interlacing stitch. Base for top stitches is similar to that of Maltese cross in interlacing (see fig. 2-117).

Figure 2-113. Skirt from Pakistan showing interlacing, feather stitch (surface embroidery) and *shi sha* glass attachment all in white thread on a blue background fabric. Courtesy of Jacqueline Enthoven.

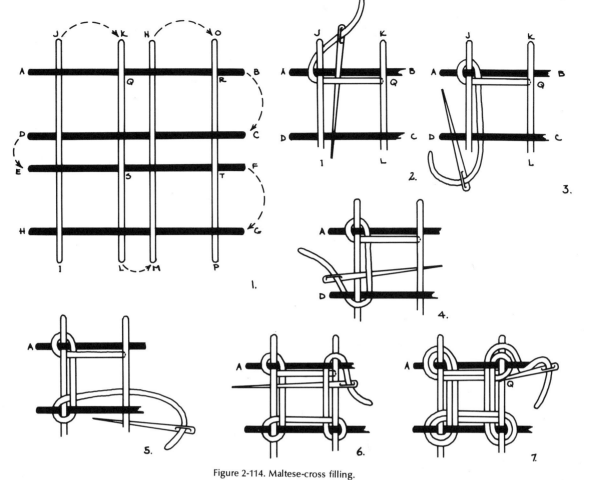

Figure 2-114. Maltese-cross filling.

Maltese-Cross Filling

Maltese-cross filling is worked on a woven plaid base of wide squares with narrow spaces between. To lay the horizontal threads, come up at A (fig. 2-114, 1). Follow the direction of the arrows, going down into the background fabric at the end of each line. End at H. Notice the spacing of the base threads in the diagram; make a wide space first, then a narrow one, and then end with a wide one.

For the verticals, begin with a new thread at I (1). Working first toward the top of the sample, weave over and then under the horizontal threads. With the same spacing as for the horizontal threads, continue to P, following the arrows and weaving alternately over and under as you go.

For the filling, begin with the large upper left-hand square. Bring the needle up through the background fabric at Q (2), under the line K L. Keeping the thread taut, weave first under the line J I, then over A B, then under J I, and again over A B. Slide the needle under the working thread, downward across the square, and under the line D C (2).

Figure 2-115. Sample of Maltese-cross filling in two colors.

97

Now you are in a position to round the second corner at the lower left. The needle goes over J I this time, under D C (3), then over J I, under the working thread, and across the square to the lower right-hand corner (4).

Complete all four corners (5, 6). Then retrace your steps around the square again to make a double woven thread (7). To finish, take the needle and thread to the back of the work at Q. Now, either with the same thread or with a new thread, perhaps of a different color, begin filling the second square by coming up at R (1).

Make the filling for each of the large squares. Work entirely on the surface threads, stitching into the background only at points Q, R, S, T (1).

Variation. Once you have learned the technique, try an all-over pattern of Maltese-cross filling in an irregularly shaped outline. Vary the colors in each alternate square for a checkerboard effect like that on the quilted turtle in Figure 2-116.

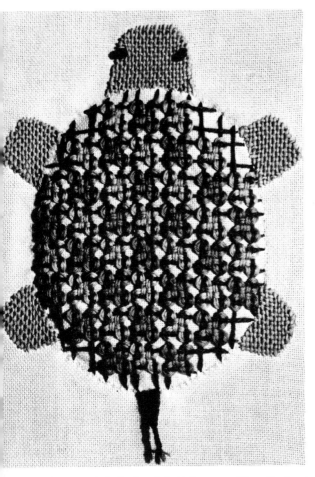

Figure 2-116. Quilted turtle in Maltese-cross filling. Head and legs are surface darning; the tail is a woven picot(see fig. 2-128).

Maltese Cross in Interlacing Stitch

The Maltese cross in interlacing stitch differs from Maltese-cross filling in that its base is made with one continuous thread rather than a series of vertical and horizontal interwoven threads. The interlacing is also worked in a continuous fashion rather than separately in each individual square.

Try the Maltese-cross filling first, as it may help you to follow this interlacing stitch, which is really one of the most complex, yet most elegant, lace stitches.

Each unit was traditionally worked in a diamond shape (fig. 2-117) then placed side by side, corners touching, to make an elaborate border.

To simplify the laying of the base threads, draw a guide with basting stitches on the background fabric (1). To do this, first make equal, crossed vertical and horizontal lines, each approximately 3 inches long. Then, begin at A (1) to make a square in the direction of the arrows. The square should bisect the arms of the cross about ½ inch from each end. End the basting at X (1).

To begin the base, come up at A (2). Go down at B, about halfway across the basted square, and come up again at C. Then make a long stitch to D parallel with the basting. Come up at E, in line with B, over to F, up again at G, down at H, and up at I. Now, go all the way across to J, but in doing so, go under the line C D. Continue to K, to L, to M, to N, and to O, thus completing the lower corner. Then from O to P, weave under the long line I J. The right corner goes from P to Q, to R, to S, to T, to U, and then weave another long stitch under O P and over C D to V. Finish the base by coming up at W and under A B to X.

In laying the base and completing the interlacing, I found that it helps to think of each corner as a separate unit. Finish each one before going on to the next.

Begin the interlacing at Y (3) with a new thread in a contrasting color. Following the diagram closely, weaving in a clockwise direction under and over the base threads, first completing the left corner, then the lower corner, then the right corner, and finally the top corner. Move from one unit to the next through the center square, continuing the interlacing carefully as you go. End at Y (4) after completing the top corner. It is exciting to see the interlacing take shape. Difficult at first, the stitching requires a little concentration but should work easily if the base threads are laid correctly. Once the stitch becomes more familiar, try several units together for a rich geometric pattern.

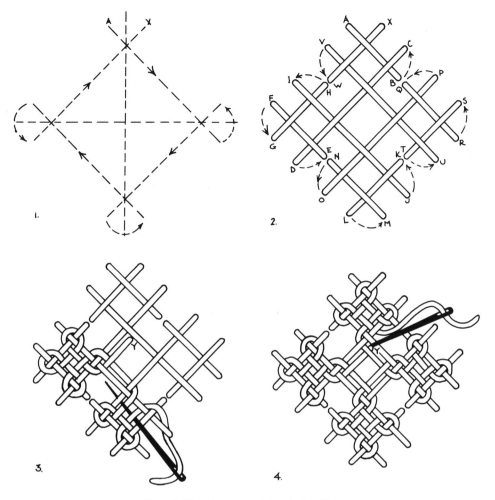

Figure 2-117. Maltese cross in interlacing stitch.

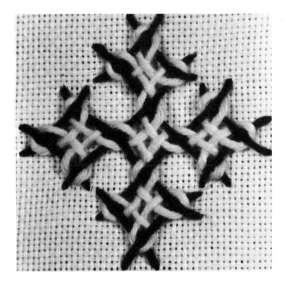

Figure 2-118. Sample of Maltese cross in interlacing stitch.

BARS

A bar is a single long thread or group of threads, attached at both ends, around which single stitches are worked to cover the base threads.

Corded, or Overcast, Bar; Twisted Bar

Corded, or overcast, bars are single threads or groups of threads attached to the background fabric at both ends and then tightly wrapped or overcast with another thread. Loosely overcast base threads are called twisted bars.

Corded bars occur frequently in traditional borders of drawn work. A section of the warp or filling threads in the background fabric is drawn or pulled out, leaving the remaining threads to be wrapped or woven. These airy and delicate patterns have become the basis for much of our contemporary needleweaving.

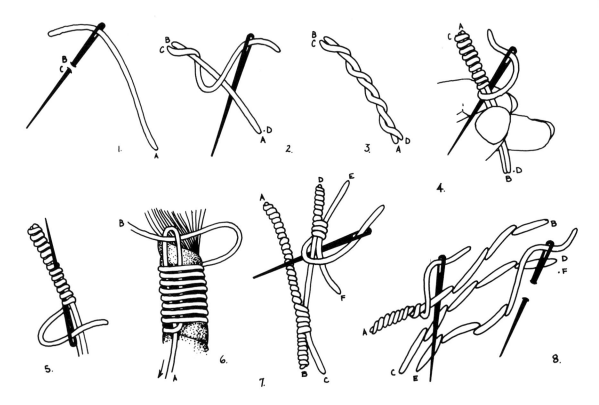

Figure 2-119. Corded, or overcast, bar.

Twisted bars. For twisted bars, the wrapping thread twists loosely around the base thread, with wide spaces between each stitch (fig. 2-119, 1, 2, and 3). For corded bars, the wrapping thread is tightly packed together, with no space between each stitch (4, 5, 7, and 8).

Make a sample, trying the twisted bar first. Come up at A (1). Pick up a little of the background fabric at B, coming up at C to begin the overcasting. Take several stitches in a clockwise direction around A B, finishing off the thread at D (2).

Corded bars. Now for the corded bar. Work a double base thread from A to B and back again to A (4). Go down in the same hole at A, coming up at C to start the overcasting. Again, overcast in a clockwise direction, but this time pack the stitches tightly together. To help keep the stitches from unraveling as you work, hold the bar between your fingers and thumb (4). If you run out of thread before completing the overcasting, loosen the last few stitches just slightly, then thread the needle back up through the overcasting and out between two stitches (5). Snip off the end of thread that sticks out. To start a new thread, reverse the process and continue the overcasting. Take the thread to the back of the work at D (4).

Whipping. For years, mariners have bound the fraying ends of their lines with whipping (6). Their technique can be borrowed by needleweavers as a finishing process for dangling ends of yarn.

Follow the steps carefully. Arrange the thread in a long loop and, starting at A, go up toward the loose ends and back down to the point where the whipping will begin. Coil the whipping very tightly around the base threads, working up toward the loop. When there are enough coils, secure the loose end (B) by threading it through the loop. Hold it in place with your thumb while pulling downward on the lower end (A). Continue pulling until the loop is hidden behind the whipping. Trim off ends A and B. The loose threads may be cut off just above the top coil or left on for a decorative fringe (see fig. 4-7).

Variation. Once familiar with the method of working a corded bar, try it on a series of long loose stitches (7: A through F). Start the overcasting to the left of A, catching in the line D C as you work. Begin again at D, catching in the line E F. The possibilities for this technique are unending. Try

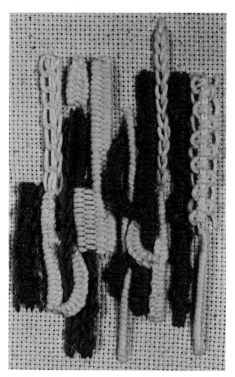

Figure 2-120. Children often make overcast bars in their work by spontaneously wrapping long, straight stitches with another thread, by Erica Nordfors at age 3.

Figure 2-121. Sampler of bars showing corded (or overcast), buttonholed, chained, and woven bars.

incorporating another color in the overcasting process, or threading more base threads over and under the existing ones.

Surface stitches may be overcast to add texture and dimension (8). Children often spontaneously overcast their stitches to make "bugs" and "lumps." Figure 2–119, 8, shows a pattern of stemstitches worked on the background fabric, then overcast.

Buttonholed Bar

A buttonholed bar is any combination of buttonhole stitches worked over a bar base. In traditional needle lace-making, sections of buttonholed bars were often used between closely worked areas to form a weblike pattern of openwork.

To work the base threads, use a medium-weight yarn such as D.M.C. Retors à Broder Cotton. Knot the thread and come up at A (fig. 2-122, 1). Making a stitch from 1 to 2 inches long, pick up a little of the background at B (1). Return to A (2), going down into the fabric in the same hole, then coming up just below A, in a position to start the buttonhole stitches.

Work buttonhole stitches in the traditional way, close together over the base threads (3). Then, later, experiment with heavier yarns, with stitches farther apart, or with stitches leaving some of the base threads showing. You will notice the stitches have a tendency to spiral around the bar, especially if the distance from A to B is more than 1 inch. You can let the twisting be a part of your design, adding interest and dimension. To do so, work about five buttonhole stitches and then, instead of making a sixth stitch, slide the needle behind the bar and out to the left (4). This will pull the stitches around the bar in a position to begin the sixth buttonhole stitch. Work to the end of the bar with groups of stitches, repeating the insertion behind the bar (4) as necessary between each group.

The base for a bar need not always be just a group of single straight stitches. Several threads may be couched to the background fabric at intervals, in any shaped design. The buttonhole stitches are worked over the base threads only, between the couching stitches (6).

For bars with buttonhole picots (7), begin at A with a thread approximately 36 inches long. Work a buttonholed bar as before (1, 2, 3). Before completing the buttonhole stitches, add more base threads in a semicircular shape. To do this, bring

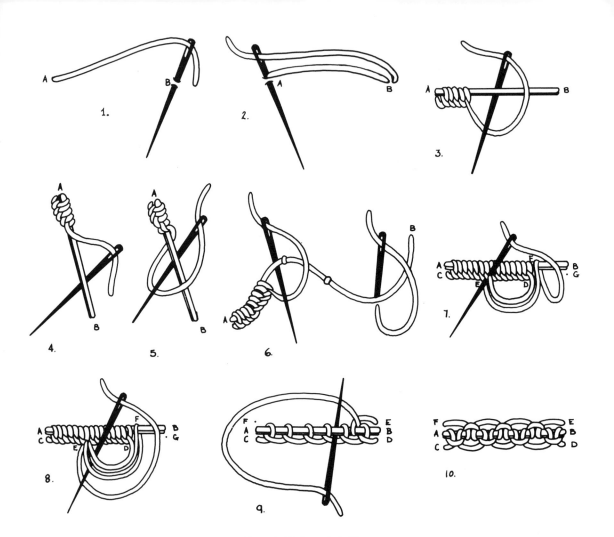

Figure 2-122. Buttonholed bar.

the working thread back toward A, below the work, and thread the needle from front to back through the base of a finished buttonhole stitch (E). Take care not to pick up any background fabric. Pull through to make a loose loop. Take the thread back to F, looping it over the bar A B, then back to the left and through the same hole as E. Adjust the three loops so they are all the same length. Begin the buttonhole stitches again in a counter-clockwise direction over these three added base threads, starting at E (8). Be sure to tighten each stitch so that it lies close to the horizontal line, by using the tip of the needle if necessary. Continue the buttonholing around the added semicircle and along the original bar to G (8).

Figure 2-123. Swan in Italian cutwork. Areas between the fabric pieces are joined with a lacy network of buttonholed bars and tiny buttonholed picots. Courtesy of The Costume and Textile Study Collection, School of Home Economics, University of Washington.

Figure 2-124. Italian needle-lace handkerchief case. The whimsical figure in detached buttonhole filling is joined to the fabric edges with buttonholed bars. Courtesy of The Costume and Textile Study Collection, School of Home Economics, University of Washington.

Buttonholed bars are equally suitable for drawn work, where the base threads are those left in the background fabric after removal of a section of either the warp or the weft (see fig. 1-25).

Variation. Try a two-sided bar by working the buttonhole stitches first in one direction, with spaces between the stitches (9: C to D). Begin the return row at E (9). Work a buttonhole stitch from below, over the bar and between each stitch of the previous row, to F (9). Or, try this technique with detached up-and-down buttonhole filling (10), also shown in Figure 2-31 and the basket (in color) on page 128.

Figure 2-125. Sample of buttonholed bars that are joined as the stitching progresses to make a diamond pattern.

Chained Bar

A single chain stitch or a square chain stitch (see below, fig. 2-126: 5, 6, 7) may be worked over a base of long straight stitches to create a raised, textured, braid-like line. Or, a detached chained bar can be made by working a single chain back into itself.

For the base of the chained bar, knot the thread and come up at A (fig. 2-126, 1). Take a small stitch in the background fabric from B to C (1), and then go back up to D. Take another small stitch at D, coming out in the same hole as A. You now have two parallel lines close together and attached at both ends.

To anchor the first chain stitch, the needle goes through the background fabric. For the remainder of the chaining, the needle goes behind the bars only. Begin the first chain by inserting the needle from above in the same hole as A (2), taking a stitch diagonally to the left and out at E (2). Make a loop with the working thread, holding it out to the left with your thumb and under the tip of the needle. Pull through to make the chain.

Work the second chain by holding the working thread to the right of the base threads. Slide the needle diagonally from the left, inside the loop of the previous stitch (3: E), not through the cloth but behind the base threads, and out over the working thread (3: F).

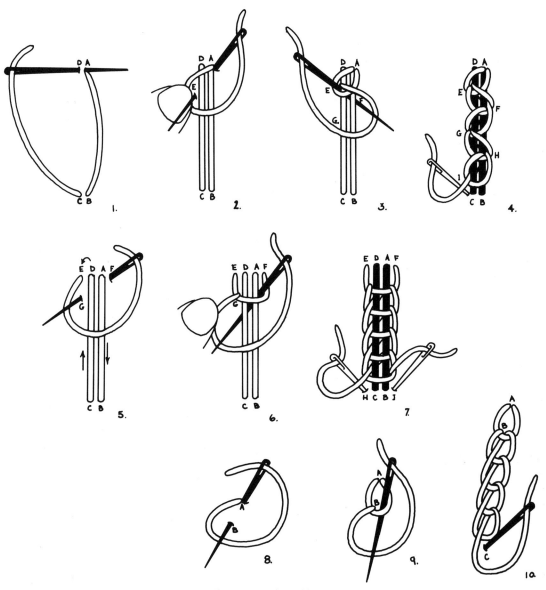

Figure 2-126. Chained bar.

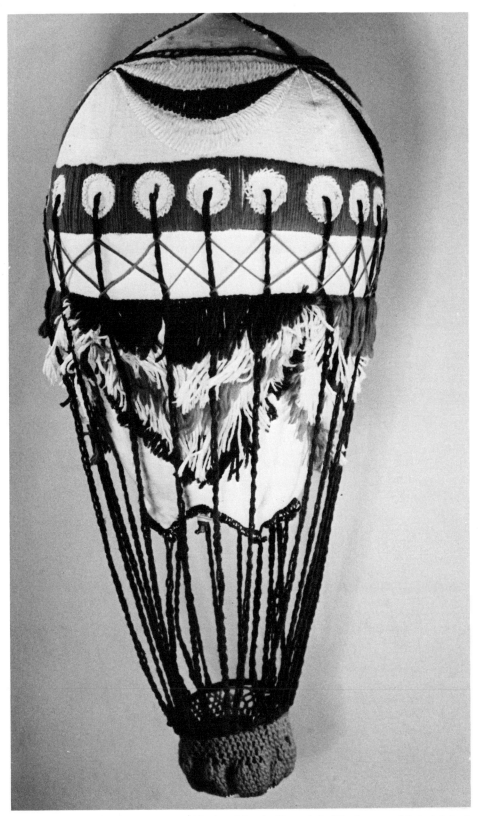

Figure 2-127. Balloon, by Vincent A. Noyes. A basket of detached buttonhole filling hangs on detached chained bars.

Repeat the first and second chain (2, 3) in this zig-zag pattern until the base threads are covered. Depending on the length of the base threads, the stitches may end on either side. Finish off the thread by going down into the background fabric in the same hole as B or C (4).

Work the base threads for the square chain as before (1) but come up at E (5) rather than A, to begin the chaining. As square chain is a wide stitch, it therefore needs more space on both sides of the bars.

Again, to anchor the first stitch, insert the needle diagonally from the right at F (5), into the fabric background, and out at G (5). Pull through gently, leaving a loose loop. Holding the working thread firmly in place with your left thumb, slide the needle over the lower right corner of the first stitch, behind the base threads, and out over the working thread (6). Again, pull through gently. Repeat (6) to cover the base threads, anchoring the working thread at H (7) when finished. Take another tack at I (7) to hold the lower right corner in place.

For a detached chained bar, no base threads are necessary. Start by making a single chain stitch into the background fabric (8). The second and succeeding stitches are worked over the loop of the previous stitch (9 and 10). Pull the stitch tight for small loops, but leave it loose for large loops. The chained bar may be free hanging or attached to the background at either end. The only limitation is the length of the working thread. When it runs out, go down into the fabric at any point (10: C).

Woven Bar, Woven Hemstitch, and Woven Picot

Woven Bar. The woven bar is a narrow base of threads bound together singly or in pairs by weaving over and under with a second thread. It can be used as the basis for other stitches. The woven hemstitch is an arrangement of woven bars that moves in a stair-step pattern from one set of base threads to the next. The Cretan open filling is worked the same way, but Cretan stitch is substituted for the weaving. A combination of woven bars and Cretan open filling, worked freely in a contemporary needleweaving design can be very effective (fig. 2-129).

To begin the woven bar, either work a series of long straight stitches on the background fabric (fig. 2-128, 1: A to H), or pull out a section of the filling threads of the background fabric to expose the warp (2).

With a new thread, come up from the back of the work between C and F (3). For a woven bar on a base of drawn-thread work, darn the loose end into the back of the fabric, and bring the needle to the front, between the threads, to begin the woven filling.

Pull the working thread to the left over B C. Slide the needle from the left, behind B C, and out to the right between C and F (3). Slide the needle from the right, behind F G, and again out between C and F. Repeat these two steps, packing the stitches together with the point of the needle as you go, until the base threads are completely covered. Go down into the background, between D and E, at the lower end of the finished bar.

Woven Hemstitch. Once familiar with the basic bar, try the woven hemstitch. Arrange a series of eight, evenly spaced, long straight stitches on the background fabric or between two fabric edges. Come up at A (4), and weave about half way down the base threads, as you did for the basic bar (3). Jump across to the middle two pairs of bars, still keeping to the under-over-under pattern of the weaving (4).

Reverse directions, and continue weaving as before, to B (5). From B, rather than taking the thread to the back of the work, thread the needle up through the completed weaving stitches to C. Secure the thread at C with a small stitch into the background fabric or hem. Begin the weaving as for A to B, hiding the thread from B to C in the work as it progresses. Work halfway down or until you meet the completed section (6). If this were a continuous border, at this point you would again jump over to the left, picking up another pair of bars and ending the weaving at D (6). Base threads remaining at the beginning or end (X), may be wrapped together as a corded or overcast bar.

Woven Picot. A description of the woven bar would not be complete without mentioning the woven picot. This funny little flat triangle is attached to the bakground only at one end, and then woven from the loose point back to the wider base. It makes good animal ears and turtle tails.

Knot the end of the thread and come up at A (7). Take a small horizontal stitch in the fabric at B, coming up at C (midway between A and B). Pull through gently, making A B into a loopy triangle. Hold the working thread from C over the point of the triangle (8). Slide the needle from the right under B, over C, and under A. Pull through gently. Move the thumbnail up to hold the point and maintain the tension, as in finishing off, below (10). Reverse the weaving, and from left go over A, under C, and over B (9). Weave back and forth to the end of the base threads. The tighter the weaving, the more rigid the triangle; it will stand up on its own or lie flat and floppy, depending on the stitching tension. Finish off the thread at the back of the work behind B (10).

Variation. Work a woven picot using a detached chain as the base (11).

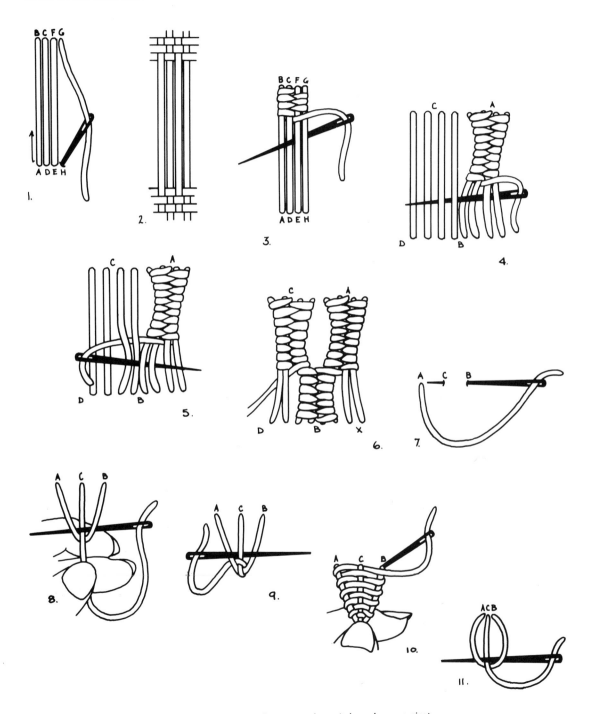

Figure 2-128. Woven bar, woven hemstitch, and woven picot.

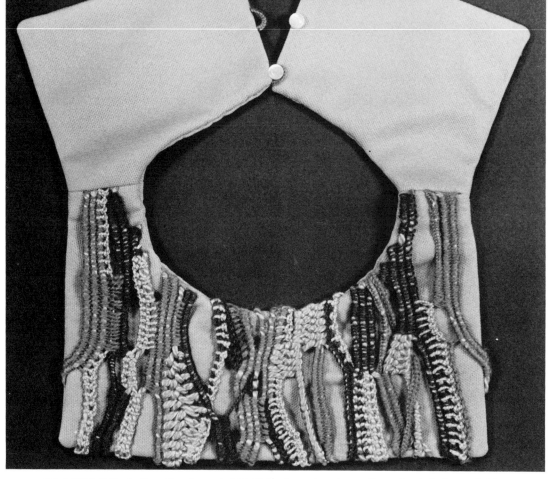

Figure 2-129. Collar, by the author. Long, straight stitches form a base for needleweaving, including corded (or overcast) bars, buttonholed bars, woven bars, Cretan open filling, and knotted buttonhole filling. Also shown in color on page 124.

Figure 2-129a. Detail of the collar.

Using the Stitches: Needle Lace & Needleweaving Combined

As you have seen, looped needle-lace stitches can make their own mesh or net when each row is worked into the preceding row. Both ends of the row must be supported in some way, either by a rigid object or a stretched fabric background. The fabric may remain as an integral part of the design or the completed lace may be cut free from the backing.

Other needle-lace stitches are stitched over or woven into a warp. A warp is any thread or group of threads held under tension by attaching the ends to a rigid object or background fabric.

If worked either on fabric, as a permanent part of the composition, or stretched across an open area, needleweaving must first have warp threads established. The filling may be any combination of stitches, but those most frequently used are surface darning, woven, corded, and buttonholed bars and Cretan open filling. These and other stitches previously described can be located quickly in the Index of Stitches at the back of the book.

There are great possibilities for present-day embroidery in the combination of needle lace and needleweaving. Artists and collectors from many parts of the United States and Canada have kindly sent me beautiful pieces of embroidery, both contemporary and traditional. By studying their photographed work and learning the stitching techniques presented here, you can find the answer to that important question: "Now that I know the stitches, what can I do with them?"

Planning the Background Fabric

DETACHED NEEDLE-LACE STITCHES

Areas of looped, detached needle-lace stitches, worked freely on a stretched fabric background, add texture to any stitchery. You can build up layers of stitches to create a third dimension (fig. 3-1). The first layer is attached to the fabric at A through H, then succeeding layers, starting at I are anchored to the stitches directly beneath. Sue

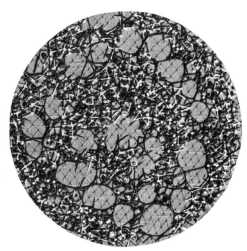

Figure 3-2. Circular composition with beads, by Susan Roach.

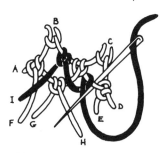

Figure 3-1. Building up stacked layers of detached stitches.

Figure 3-3. *Norman Castle*, wall hanging in hand-dyed yarns, using surface embroidery stitches with areas of detached buttonhole filling, by Flo Wilson.

Roach uses this stacking technique in a round composition (fig. 3-2). Machine-made netting covered a stretched background fabric as a base for several contrasting layers of double buttonhole filling. Tiny ceramic beads were incorporated in the stitchery. The net in this case was simply an onion bag, stretched with the background material, giving a little more texture than the fabric alone. The netting was not obvious after the layers of double buttonhole filling were worked.

Try a combination of detached fillings with basic surface-embroidery stitches. Beginning stitchery students usually learn herringbone and running stitch, French knots and couching. Flo Wilson, in her whimsical *Norman Castle* (fig. 3-3), combines these familiar stitches with raised areas of detached buttonhole filling.

A net of looped detached stitches need not always be flat or layered on the fabric background. In *Anywhere that's Wild* (fig. 3-4), Wilcke Smith uses detached buttonhole filling to make "small stuffed limpet forms in fine wool" and "two nests to hide secrets in." For more ideas, see pages 24-30.

STITCHING ON LAID THREADS

As mentioned, looped detached stitches can make their own net if each row is worked back into the preceding row. Another way to attach these stitches to the background fabric is to establish a warp of laid threads on the cloth, as described on page 20. Looped and woven stitches are then built up on this base. The laid threads can be random or planned, freely worked on the fabric with no boundaries or contained by a visual or stitched outline. Build up a heavy, raised area, fill in a flat area, visually extend a design motif, attach a bead or a piece of glass — you can do all this with laid threads or long straight stitches. Experiment with color, texture, and weight of yarns, both for the base threads and the overstitching.

There are very few set rules for stitching on laid threads. Take any stitch out of its traditional context, and see what it will do. Make stitches bigger, smaller, thicker, flatter, weave them over or under other stitches. Each time you try a new approach, it will suggest another idea.

Random Warp

There is a very free feeling about picking up a piece of cloth, stretching it on a frame or hoop, and then with no plans at all — just a wisp of an idea — starting to stitch. Working detached stitches on a random warp of laid threads also can

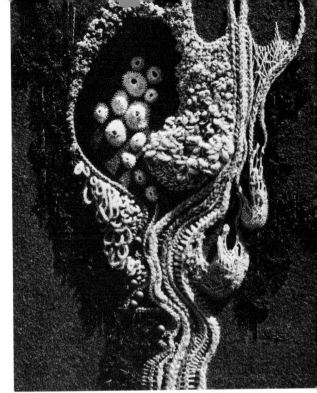

Figure 3-4. *Anywhere That's Wild,* by Wilcke Smith. Detached buttonhole filling makes raised forms and nets that can be stuffed or used to put things in. Photograph by Bob Smith.

Figure 3-5. Composition in buttonholed bars on random warp threads, by Mary Ann Spawn. Also shown in color on page 121.

give you this feeling. Let your idea develop as the stitching progresses.

Mary Ann Spawn's composition in buttonholed bars is made on raised warp threads held away from the cloth at one end by a bead (fig. 3-5). Other laid threads are flat on the surface of the

Figure 3-6. Stuffed doll figure, by Joan Lewis, decorated with buttonholed and woven bars.

Figure 3-8. Butterfly, by Carol Weyhrich, done in two sizes of D.M.C. Perle Cotton in detached buttonhole stitches that make their own random warp.

cloth, and all are covered with the same buttonhole stitch (see detail, in color, on page 121.)

The stuffed doll figure (fig. 3-6) by Joan Lewis is dressed in buttonholed and woven bars. Laid base threads are created by extending the working thread across the fabric after completing the last stitch in each row (fig. 3-7). This method is a more freely worked version of the buttonholed half-bar insertion.

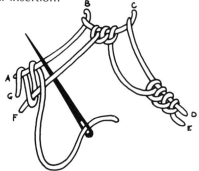

Figure 3-7. Laid base threads, as in Figure 3-6, are created by extending the working thread across the fabric after completing the last stitch in each row.

This same technique fills the butterfly's wings in Figure 3-8. The oval areas are outlined on the fabric background in buttonhole stitch. After filling with detached buttonhole on a random warp, the cloth behind is cut away. The same stitching, in a contrasting color, visually extends the inner open areas to the outer line of the wings.

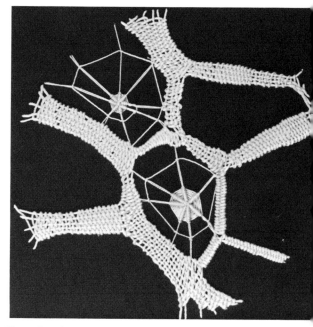

Figure 3-9. An exercise in needleweaving and raised-stem spiderweb stitch, by the author.

In Figure 3-9, a random warp is arranged on a fabric stretched in a 6-inch embroidery hoop. Groups of threads are gathered in flat lines of weaving and woven bars. A separate warp for raised-stem spiderweb stitches is worked in the open spaces.

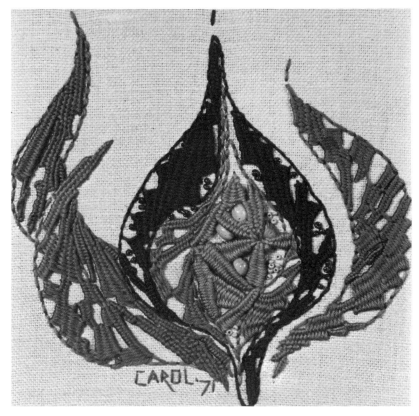

Figure 3-10. Framed needleweaving, by Carol Weyhrich. The random raised and flat warp threads are enclosed in an outline of backstitch.

Figure 3-11. Framed needleweaving, by Eugenia Duffy. Warp threads left in the knee of a pair of blue jeans when the filling wore out form the base for corded and woven bars.

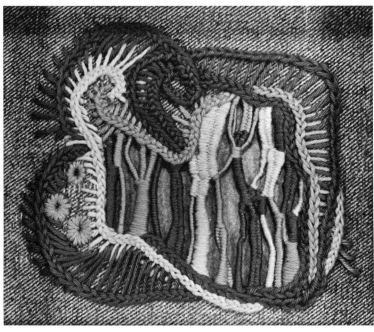

Freely stitched random warp threads for needleweaving and detached stitches are often confined to filling a more specific area. You may want to draw an outline with running stitches in sewing thread, which will be removed when the work is finished. Or, make the outline a permanent part of the design by using backstitch, chain stitch or couching. Explore other surface-embroidery stitches for outlining possibilities, such as the Vandyke stitch in Figure 3-11, which creates a rich free-flowing border.

Carol Weyrich found that a gnarled piece of driftwood served as an inspiration for her needleweaving (fig. 3-12). The stitches are arranged in clusters on the background fabric, to conform to the shape of the wood. Beads, like grains of sand, are nestled into its cracks and holes.

A random warp is contained in a 2½-inch border strip down the front of a vest by the author. (detail, fig. 3-13). Flat woven areas and corded and woven bars combine with beads, French knots (a well-known surface-embroidery stitch) and a wrapped fringe (see detail, in color, on page 125.)

Random warp threads, covered with decorative stitches, are perfect for attaching objects to a background fabric. A delicate web holds pieces of glass in Eleanor Van de Water's *Autumn Arabesque* (fig. 3-16). In *Sea Forest* (fig. 3-17) by Wilcke Smith, long straight stitches held up in the center by a bead, make a circular random warp for Cretan stitch.

Figure 3-12. Needleweaving, by Carol Weyrich. Clusters of woven areas and beads conform to a shape inspired by a piece of driftwood.

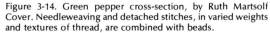

Figure 3-13. Vest, detail, by the author. Two and-a-half-inch bands of needleweaving stretch from shoulder seam to hemline at the front opening. Courtesy of Mrs. Earl Chalk.

Figure 3-14. Green pepper cross-section, by Ruth Martsolf Cover. Needleweaving and detached stitches, in varied weights and textures of thread, are combined with beads.

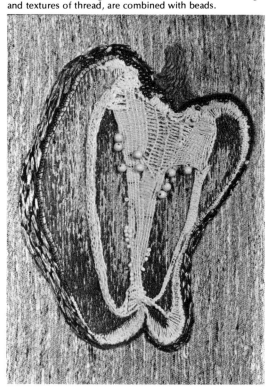

Figure 3-15. *Rain Forest*, suede and Swedish wool by the author. Random warp threads form a base for Cretan open filling and woven, corded, and buttonholed bars.

Figure 3-16. *Autumn Arabesque,* by Eleanor Van de Water. Buttonholed and woven bars hold pieces of glass to the fabric surface.

Figure 3-17. *Sea Forest,* by Wilcke Smith. Straight stitches, raised in the center with a bead, form a circular warp for Cretan open filling. The wrapped, undulating lines are corded bars. Photograph by Bob Smith. Also shown in color on page 124.

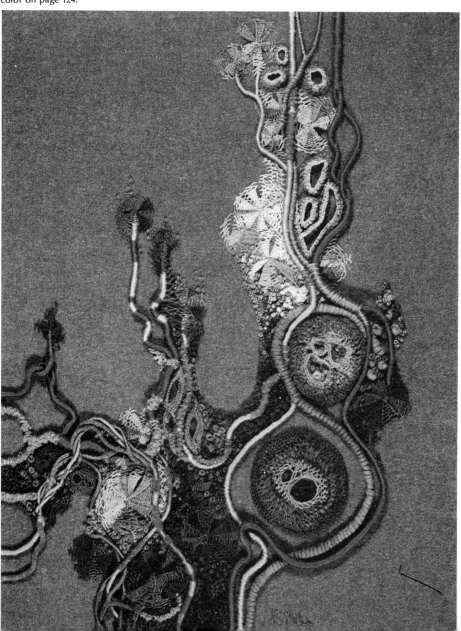

Figure 3-18. Carol Weyhrich combines both layered and flat needleweaving with areas of double and knotted buttonhole filling.

Figure 3-19. Appliqué with needleweaving, by the author. Circular cut-outs of tie-bleached fabric are appliquéd with a planned warp of long straight stitches.

Figure 3-19a. Detail of the needleweaving and appliquéd circles in Figure 3-19.

Planned Warp

In a planned warp for detached stitches, the threads are usually evenly spaced in a repeated pattern. They are arranged singly or in groups to conform to a specific shape, as in Figure 2-70. Both random and planned warps can be combined. Carol Weyhrich's combination of layered weaving on a random warp with an outer rim of planned warp (fig. 3-18) visually extends the inner circular shape. The centers are filled with nets of double and knotted buttonhole filling done in novelty yarn.

In Figure 3-19, circles of black cloth are tie-bleached to remove the color. A solution of one part bleach to one part water works well for this purpose. Raylike stitches are used to appliqué the circles to the background, and at the same time form a warp for needleweaving. The woven filling echoes the black fabric areas, making a transition of pattern from the circle to the background.

STITCHING ON DRAWN THREADS

Sections of warp or filling threads can be drawn or pulled out of a piece of cloth, leaving some threads exposed (see page 17.) These exposed threads, like laid threads on the surface of the fabric, can make a warp for detached stitches and needleweaving.

In some traditional drawn-thread work borders, exposed threads were bound together in groups to make the woven hemstitch. Figure 3-20 shows an ornate example of this on fine linen, all stitched in gold threads. For a more contemporary approach (fig. 3-21), Eleanor Van de Water weaves warp threads together in groups with woven hemstitch, and woven and corded bars. For textural interest, she has incorporated hanks of red hair in the weaving, and left the pulled out threads dangling as a fringe.

Figure 3-20. Traditional drawn-thread work border on a square of fine linen, with a woven filling of gold threads. Courtesy of Marge Krejcik.

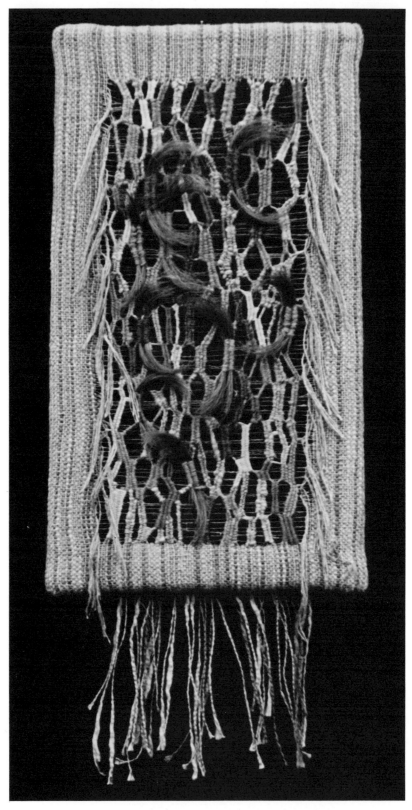

Figure 3-21. *Mama's Red-Haired Boy is Gone*, Needleweaving on drawn-thread work, by Eleanor Van de Water, incorporating hanks of red hair.

Detail of composition in buttonholed bars, by Mary Ann Spawn. Full piece is shown in Figure 3-5.

Great-Grandmother's Bottom Drawer, sampler of needle lace, *by the author. Shapes include a hat, belt, pincushion, vest, button-box, mirror, and purse.*

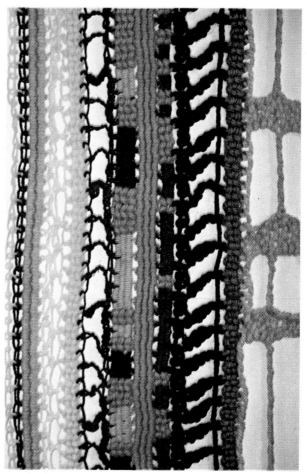

Hanging (detail), strips of macramé joined with needle-lace stitches, by Flo Wilson.

Lassie Wittman pulled out some threads from a loosely woven casement fabric to make a base fabric (fig. 3-22). Rather than discard these threads, she used them to stitch the remaining warp in pleasing combinations of weaving and buttonholed and corded bars.

Contrast between solid areas of cloth and open linear spaces of stitching is one of the most appealing aspects of drawn-thread work. To create this effect, pull out threads in any pattern you choose, leaving some of the fabric background intact. For ways of binding the edges of the open areas, or hiding loose ends of threads, see Figure 1-23. Maggie Turner hides cut fabric edges with masses of French knots (fig. 3-23) and wraps the remaining warp threads as for corded or overcast bars. The finished piece is mounted in an embroidery hoop, set away from a fabric backing, for a rich shadow pattern.

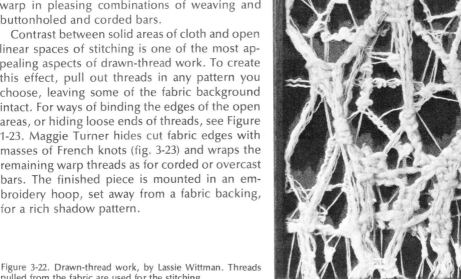

Figure 3-22. Drawn-thread work, by Lassie Wittman. Threads pulled from the fabric are used for the stitching.

Figure 3-23. Drawn-thread work by Maggie Turner. Exposed threads are wrapped as for corded bars.

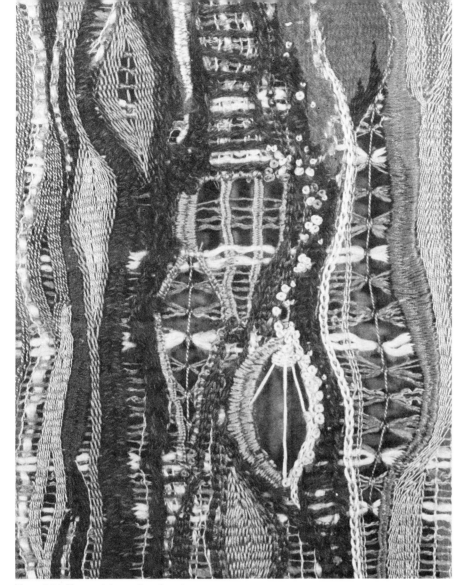

Figure 3-24. Textured drawn-thread work by Beverly Rush.

Figure 3-25. Delicate traditional needle lace. Most of the warp and filling threads are removed, then remaining threads are gathered with weaving and coral knots. Courtesy of Ada King.

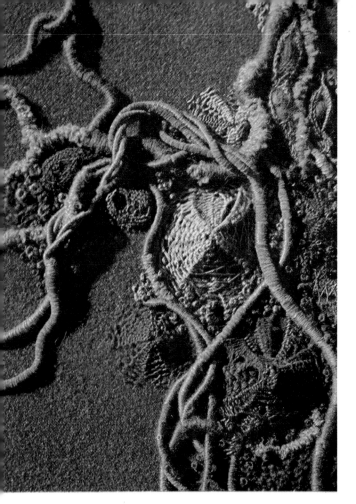

Left: Sea Forest (detail), by Wilcke Smith. Photo by Bob Smith. Full piece is shown in Figure 3-17. Below: Needleweaving (detail), wool and cotton yarns with suede circles, by the author. Photo by Beverly Rush.

Collar, needleweaving, by the author. Courtesy of Mrs. B. Nordfors. The full piece is shown in Figure 2-129.

Right: *Borders of needleweaving on a vest, by the author.* Below: *Framed needleweaving, by Mary Ann Spawn.*

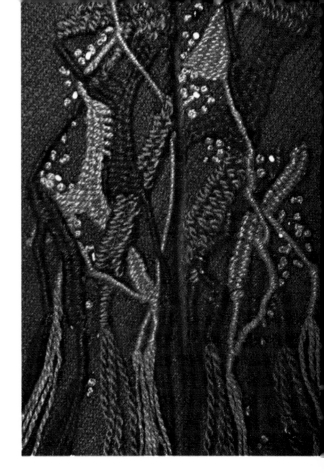

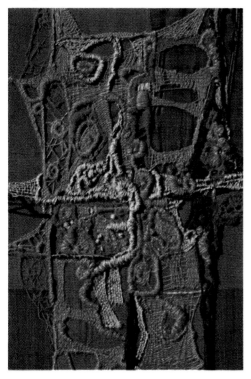

Needle lace fills areas between heavy, wrapped ropes, by Flo Wilson. Photo by artist.

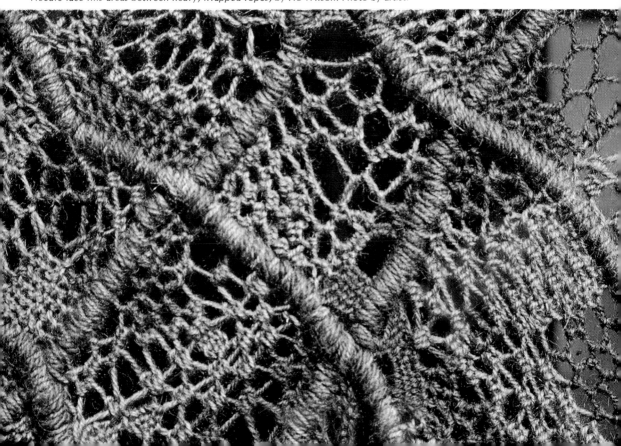

Stitching Free from Background Fabric

DETACHED NEEDLE-LACE STITCHES

Rows of detached looped stitches can be free from any background fabric, without supporting warp threads. The beginning and end of each row is instead held in place with other stitches, or some rigid object such as an embroidery hoop, wooden frame, metal ring, heavy rope or even an old umbrella skeleton.

Once you have learned the stitches in their traditional way, worked in evenly spaced uniform rows, you can work freely, distorting the stitches by making them larger or smaller and experimenting with various weights and textures of yarn.

Flo Wilson combines needle lace and macramé in a colorful hanging of hand-dyed four-ply wool (fig. 3-27). Macramé strips are joined with spaced buttonhole filling, lacy buttonhole filling, bands of detached buttonhole filling, and overcast bars. No warp threads are necessary, as the macramé strips are firm enough to support the netlike stitches. To make the joining process easier, the strips are anchored to a foam rubber slab with large T-pins placed perpendicular to the work and approximately 2 inches apart.

Pat Albiston found an unused inner ring of a 6-inch embroidery hoop. The outer ring had been broken and discarded. She covered the hoop in a knitting worsted with tight buttonhole stitches, as

Figure 3-26. *Foam*, needle-lace hanging, by Virginia Churchill Bath. Photograph by the artist.

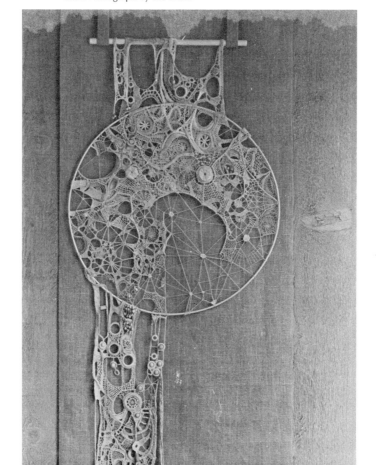

Figure 3-27. Hanging (detail), by Flo Wilson, combining needle lace and macramé. Also shown in color on page 121.

for the buttonholed bar (fig. 3-28). The stitches form a ridge around the inside of the circle to use as an anchor for knotted buttonhole stitches worked in fine metallic threads and knitting worsted. Delicate glass beads are threaded on the needle as the stitching progresses. Beads about ¾ inch in diameter have holes large enough to take the needle. Solid areas of plain over-and-under weaving add contrast to the open areas.

Irene Ouska uses hoops in another way (figs. 3-29 and 3-30). A three-dimensional sculptured sphere of soldered brass forms the base for her needle-lace stitches. Some warp threads are necessary for the buttonholed and woven bars, but most of the stitches are in rows, suspended between the brass arcs. The mingled stitches are: Ceylon stitch, lacy buttonhole filling, couching with buttonhole stitch, double buttonhole filling, and detached up-and-down buttonhole filling.

Evelyn Svec Ward, in her hanging *Fiber Screen II*, (fig. 3-31) works stitches around a wooden frame, into other stitches and into areas of knitting. The work is composed mainly of detached buttonhole stitch and Cretan stitch with rich textural interest created by the use of varied threads, sisal, cotton, burlap, and chenille.

Beverly Switzer cleverly combines macramé and lacy buttonhole filling between the spokes of an umbrella frame (figs. 3-32 and 3-32a). Macramé knots often correspond to stitches in needle lace. For example, in Figure 3-32a, one of the spokes is wrapped in twisting half hitches. This same effect can be made by stitching a twisted buttonholed bar.

A gnarled Manzanita branch supports rows of lacy buttonhole filling worked in heavy white cord by Luana Sever (fig. 3-33). Contrasting solid areas of leather are stretched between the branches and laced in place with the same white cord.

Detail of Feuervogel (Firebird) by Barbara Meier. The full piece is shown in Figure 3-46.

White Birds, framed hanging in needleweaving and spider-web techniques, by Wilcke Smith. Photo by Bob Smith.

Basket, hand-dyed yarns in buttonholed bars, by Flo Wilson.

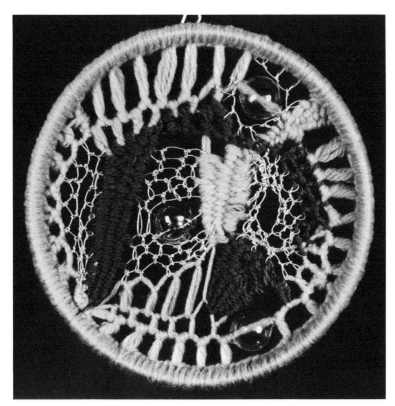

Figure 3-28. A 6-inch embroidery hoop supports knotted buttonhole stitches, needleweaving, and glass beads, by Pat Albiston.

Figure 3-29. A 4-inch hanging sphere supports needle-lace stitches, by Irene Ouska.

Figure 3-30. A 6-inch hanging sphere of soldered brass rings supports needle-lace stitches and beads, by Irene Ouska.

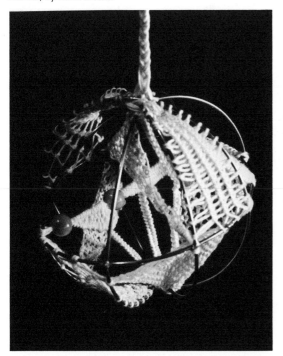

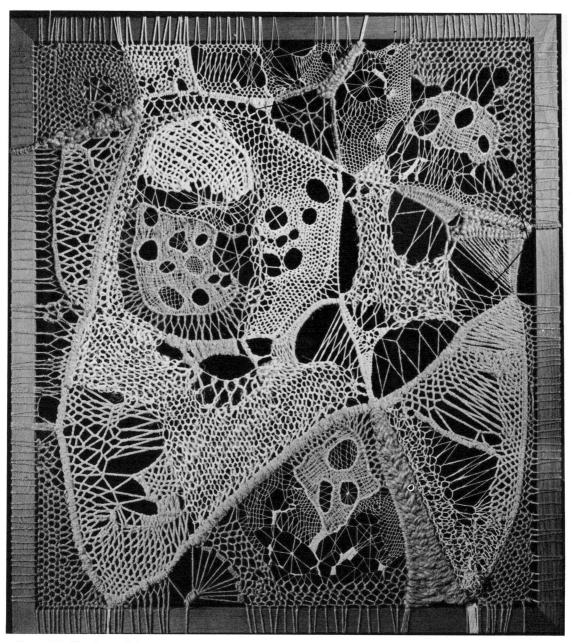

Figure 3-31. *Fiber Screen II,* hanging panel in needle lace and knitting by Evelyn Svec Ward. Photograph by William E. Ward.

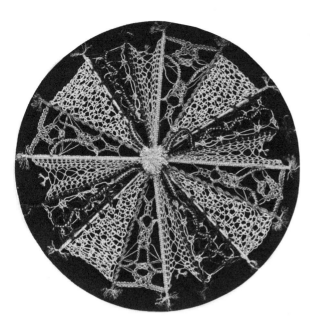

Above: Figure 3-32. Spokes of an old umbrella frame support a combination of needle lace and macramé in bright jute cords, by Beverly J. Switzer.

Right: Figure 3-32a. Detail of the umbrella.

Below: Figure 3-33. A gnarled Manzanita branch supports rows of lacy buttonhole filling and areas of leather, by Luana Sever. Photograph by Robert S. Newton.

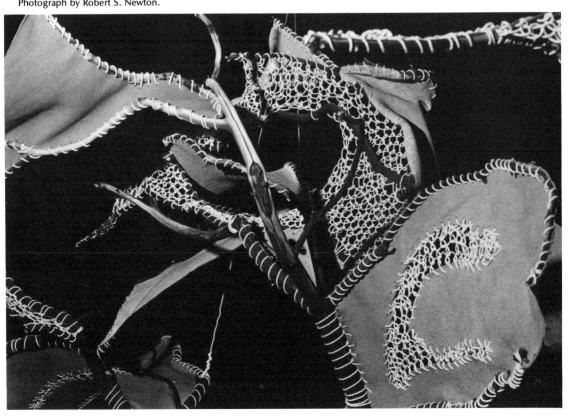

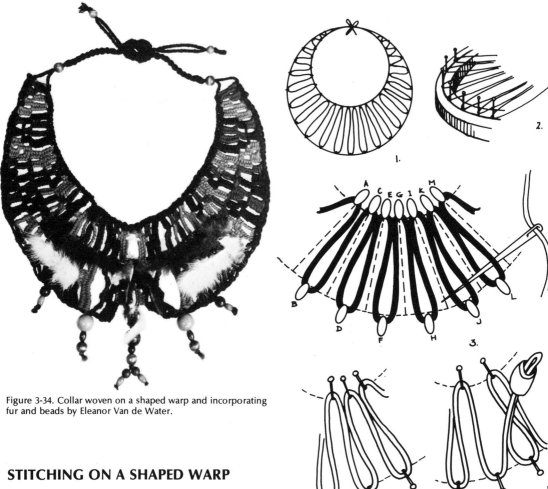

Figure 3-34. Collar woven on a shaped warp and incorporating fur and beads by Eleanor Van de Water.

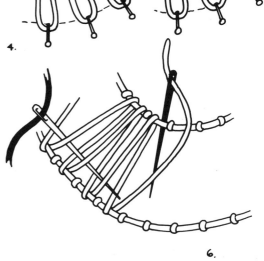

Figure 3-35. Ways of setting up warp threads for a shaped weaving.

STITCHING ON A SHAPED WARP

A shaped warp is a series of evenly spaced parallel threads, conforming to any shape, and held under tension around the outline by pins, couched threads, or single stitches.

Collars and Neckpieces

Eleanor Van de Water weaves collars and neckpieces on shaped warps (fig. 3–34). Yarn, fur, and beads are combined on a warp stretched between two embroidery hoops tied together, one 6 inches in diameter and one 10 inches (fig. 3-35, 1). She places straight pins with small round colored heads into the groove of each hoop, ⅛ inch apart on the inner circle and ½ inch apart on the outer circle (2). Colored pins stand out from the weaving so there is no chance of losing them in the work.

The same type of warp may be set up by drawing any shape on a paper pattern, then sticking pins through the outline of the pattern and into a slab of foam rubber (4). To hold the warp threads more firmly, angle the pins away from the pattern almost in a horizontal position.

The warp threads must be strong and should have enough body to help the finished piece maintain its shape. Linen rug warp, available from weaving suppliers, or a twisted cotton macramé cord are both good choices. Ordinarily, the warp will be covered as the woven filling progresses. If you prefer to leave some threads exposed as part of the design, be sure to choose a compatible yarn color.

To string beads on the warp, at random, before beginning the filling, remove one pin and slide the bead over the double thread (fig. 3-35, 5).

Shaped warps can also be set up by borrowing traditional lace-maker's techniques. Pin or baste the paper pattern to a stretched fabric background. Outline the area in one of two ways, either with small stitches (3), or with a heavy couched thread (6). In each case, when the work is finished, remove it from the backing by clipping the small anchoring stitches.

When the warp is set up, begin the filling by weaving two or three rows of plain weave (over one, under one) around the edges with a tapestry needle. Pack these rows in tightly with the needle tip or a pronged table fork. Then, fill the remaining area, using a variety of stitches, yarns, and materials. Experiment with textured and novelty yarns. Incorporate beads, shells, feathers, or leather. Extra warp threads may be added as the work progresses by working long straight stitches over a finished area.

In Figures 3-34 and 3-36 the stitches are woven and corded bars. Try other stitches worked closely together, such as the Cretan open filling or knotted buttonhole filling.

Teneriffe Lace

Teneriffe lace originated from an ancient Spanish needle-lace technique popular in the sixteenth century, and later practiced by the Latin American peoples.

Individual star, sun, or flower-like motifs, woven and knotted on a circular warp, are joined to each other by separate stitches to make one large piece of lace. Studying the designs of these delicate weavings can be an inspiration for many ideas in contemporary embroidery (see page 8).

You may want to appliqué a single decorative medallion to a dress or work the lace on a warp stretched across a cut-out area. To learn the basic technique, make a 3-inch circle in D.M.C. Retors à Broder Cotton, or D.M.C. Perle Cotton size 3. Then go on to try large circles in bulky yarn or very small circles in fine thread.

At first, Teneriffe lace was made with the aid of a pillow and pins to hold the warp in place. Later, metal devices in various shapes with sawtooth edges took the place of the pillow. Today we can replace the traditional pillow with a foam-rubber slab, pinning the warp in a circle as for the shaped collar already described (fig. 3-35, 4). When pins are arranged close together in a small circle, they are difficult to work around and tend

Figure 3-36. Collar on a shaped warp filled with woven bars and beads, in wool and novelty yarns, by Eleanor Van de Water.

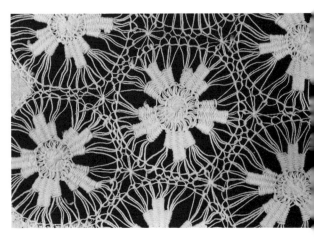

Figure 3-37. Circles of Teneriffe lace are joined by separate stitches to make one large piece of lace. Courtesy of Beverly Rush.

to catch the thread. Figure 3-39 demonstrates a way to hold the warp with backstitches, which I like better than pins.

To make the sample, outline a circle on a stretched fabric by tracing around a jar lid, glass, or cup. Work a series of backstitches around the perimeter. For a woven center, there must be an odd number of outlining backstitches (1). For a knotted center, where groups of threads are tied together with coral knots, you can have either an odd or an even number.

When the outline is complete, thread the needle with a long thread, tie a knot in the end, and come up in the center at X (2). Slide the

Figure 3-38. Traditional motif from a Teneriffe-lace tablecloth. Courtesy of Mrs. Paulen W. Kaseberg.

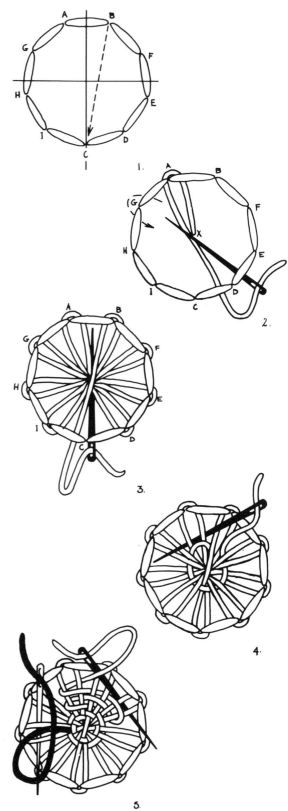

needle from below, under the stitch A B, then from above, under the stitch A G, being careful not to pick up any background fabric. Take the needle and thread to the lower edge of the circle across X, then slide it from above under the stitch CD, and from below under the stitch D E. This completes one figure eight. Make the next loop at G and the opposite loop at E. Continue the figure eights all around the circle, moving over one stitch each time (3). On the last loop, thread the needle under the lumpy center section, coming up between the spokes in a position to start the woven filling. Weave two or three times around the center counterclockwise, alternately over and under the pairs of threads. Pack the weaving in tightly with the tip of the needle (4).

End the thread by weaving it back through and hiding it in the center section. Snip off excess thread. To start a new thread, poke the needle through the center. Then, thread it through the woven section toward the outer rim of the circle to resume the stitching. To join threads, use the tiny weaver's knot (see fig. 1-59), being careful to hide it in the underside of the work.

Finish the filling by dividing the warp into equal sections, and then weaving toward the outer edge of the circle to make petals or rays. Add smaller circles within the larger one by tying each pair of warp threads together with a coral knot (5). Figure 3-40 illustrates the use of Teneriffe-lace filling techniques on a crossed warp similar to the one used for raised-stem spiderweb stitch.

When the circle is finished, remove it from the cloth backing after clipping the outlining backstitches and the knot in the back at X.

Figure 3-39. Teneriffe-lace circles.

134

Figure 3-40. Sample of Teneriffe-lace filling techniques on a crossed warp, as for raised-stem spiderweb stitch.

STITCHING ON A DETACHED WARP

A detached warp is like a fringe anchored at one end and hanging free at the other. The tension needed to work the filling is created by holding onto the free end with one hand, while stitching

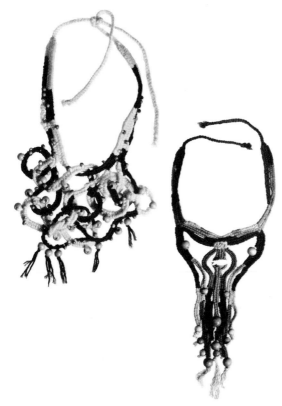

Figures 3-41, 3-42. Woven necklaces with beads, by Eleanor Van de Water.

with the other. The most successful way of fastening one end of the warp while working on the loose end is pinning with T-pins stuck at an angle into a foam-rubber slab. Eleanor Van de Water makes unusual and ornate necklaces using this technique (fig. 3-41 and 3-42).

For a necklace base or warp, use linen rug warp, navy cord, or any fairly stiff twisted cord, to give body to the finished piece. As previously mentioned, if the warp is not to be completely covered, the color of the cord becomes important. Cut five cords, each 60 inches long, and mark the center with yarn tie A (fig. 3-43, 1).

To determine the size of the neck opening, hold the cords with the point A at the center front of the neck. Drape the cords loosely around to the center back, then mark this point with yarn tie B (2). Mark C with a yarn tie that is as far from A as A is from B. Bring the loose ends of cord back around to the front. They eventually will form the more ornate part of the necklace.

Yarns for the weaving should not be too fine, as the work becomes tedious and the warp threads will show through. Select three to four colors in a four-ply wool and coordinating beads with holes large enough to take several threads. Beads can also be sewn on with a separate thread after the necklace is finished.

Start the weaving at B (3), where the cords are doubled back to form a loop. Anchor the loop to a piece of foam rubber with a T-pin. Divide the ten cords into groups of three, four, and three. With a tapestry needle, start weaving from the middle of the cords toward the outside edge, over and under the groups of warp threads. Pull the working thread through, leaving a 4- to 6-inch tail to use later for covering the looped ends of the exposed warp. Return the needle and thread to the neck edge, by weaving alternating over and under below the first row. Continue weaving toward point A, using the tip of the needle to pack the filling yarn tightly together as you go (4).

To end the first color, take the working thread to the back of the necklace, and slide the needle up through the woven portion. Pull through and snip off the end. Start a new color the same way, but in the reverse direction, threading the needle down toward the area to be woven.

At any point, you may change the weaving to a separate group of warp threads (5). Add beads during the work by sliding them on the loose ends and up toward B (5). Relieve the areas of solid weaving by incorporating buttonholed and corded bars and any other stitches you may wish to experiment with. When the filling from B comes within 1½ inches of A, start filling the area between C and A. When the two sides are finished, plan the front section. More warp

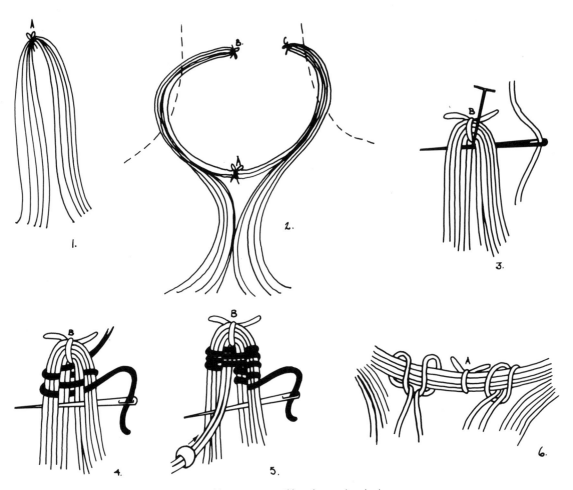

Figure 3-43. Making a woven necklace from a detached warp.

threads can be attached at A, or to the woven sides, if necessary (6).

When the necklace is finished, cover dangling warp ends with close-set twisted buttonhole stitches or beads, or fray them to make a tassel. A drop of white glue will keep buttonhole stitches from sliding off the end of the warp. For a fastening, attach a bead at C and a buttonholed loop at B.

Voski Chakirian Sprague has created an exquisite cape, combining macramé, feathers, needlelace stitches, and beads (figs. 3-45 and 3-45a). Ends of heavy cords falling from the shoulder line provide a detached warp for Cretan open filling and buttonholed bars. Tiny groups of detached buttonhole stitches hold the beads in place, others are tied on to loose ends of the stitching yarn.

Figure 3-44. Woven necklace in wool yarn and twisted buttonhole fringe, with unglazed clay beads, by the author.

Figure 3-45. Cape, detached warp of heavy cord in Cretan stitch, and buttonholed bars, with guinea-hen feathers and beads, by Voski Chakirian Sprague.

Figure 3-45a. Detail of the cape.

Figure 3-46. *Feuervogel* (Firebird), hanging by Barbara Meier. Also shown in color on page 128.

Barbara Meier has developed a technique of weaving strips on a narrow detached warp, with a needle, in vibrant colored wool yarns. (fig. 3-46; see detail fig. 4-7 and detail, in color, on page 128.) As each strip progresses, it is pinned in the shape of the design to a piece of insulation board. Subsequent strips are partially joined to the first strips, eventually making a deeply layered texture. The ends of warp are whipped in sections of brilliant color, and the finished piece is hung from a heavy wire threaded through the back of the work.

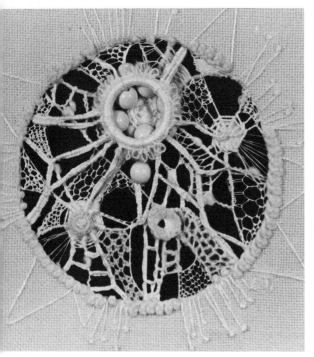

Figure 3-47. *Moon Crater II*, needle lace on random warp threads, stretched in a circular cut-out mat, by Virginia S. Thorne.

Figure 3-48. Border of a white eyelet kerchief from Bohemia. Needle-lace motifs are stitched between the edges of cut-out areas. Courtesy of The Costume and Textile Study Collection, School of Home Economics, University of Washington.

STITCHING ON A STRETCHED WARP

A stretched warp is a series of random or evenly spaced threads stretching across an open area and held under tension at both ends. The means of supporting the threads remains as a permanent part of the finished work.

Random Warp

Virginia Thorne makes delicate compositions of needle lace on a random warp stretched across a circular cut-out area (fig. 3-47). Cut a circle out of a piece of heavy cardboard, and then cover the cardboard with fabric as shown in Figure 1-32. The fabric then serves as both a permanent background and a means of anchoring ends of warp and filling threads around the circle's perimeter. The lace stitches in Figure 3-47 are tulle stitch, lacy, knotted, and double buttonhole filling, Cretan stitch, buttonholed bars, Ceylon stitch, plain over-and-under weaving, and raised-stem spiderweb stitch. Straight stitches and French knots spill over onto the background, making a pleasing transition from open space to solid fabric.

Carol Weyhrich stretches a random warp around a small square frame (fig. 3-49). The warp is completely engulfed by stitches that combine heavily textured novelty yarns with beads, in needleweaving (over and under several warp threads) and buttonhole stitches. The lack of set rules in random warps allows you freedom of creativity, and the design evolves as you work the areas of filling stitches. Add more warp, as necessary, around the frame as the stitching progresses.

There are countless ways to support stretched warp threads. Carolyn Doughton uses nails with a loosely woven decorative fabric on a slab of weathered driftwood (fig. 3-50). Distorted lengthwise threads echo the wavy lines of the wood grain. Warp threads strung with clay beads are stretched between nails arranged in a random pattern. The knot hole in the driftwood is left uncovered as a center of interest. For contrast, some areas of the linear warping are filled in with solid needleweaving, and buttonholed and woven bars.

Figure 3-48a. Detail of a different section of the kerchief in Figure 3-48.

Figure 3-49. Needleweaving, by Carol Weyhrich. Random warp threads are stretched around a small wood frame.

Figure 3-50. Needleweaving, by Carolyn Doughton. Warp threads are stretched on driftwood between nails.

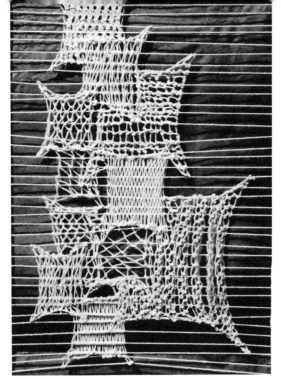

Figure 3-51. A high-school student's framed abstract in needle lace on a stretched warp, by Robin Osteo. Photograph by Jacqueline Enthoven.

Spaced Warp

In a spaced warp the stretched threads are set up in a repeat pattern, either singly or in groups, allowing for more deliberate planning than is called for in a random warp.

Jacqueline Enthoven, working with Sister Betty Paquin, head of the art department at Holy Names Academy, Seattle, Washington, devised a needle-lace project for high-school freshmen (figs. 3-51 and 3-52). The students, Robin Osteo and Colleen Lynch, first stretched evenly spaced warp threads through holes drilled in a frame (see fig. 1-29). A paper pattern with a drawn design was then taped behind the warp threads. The main areas were outlined in coral knots and then filled in with needle-lace stitches. When Colleen's cat was finished, there was too much empty space around it, which was quickly and cleverly remedied by tying the exposed warp threads in groups to make a patterned background.

Merry Bean worked *Summertime* (fig. 3-53) on warp threads spaced 1 inch apart and stretched on a frame. She made the piece to hang in a window so, ". . . you can see through the silhouette of the work in the daytime, while at night it becomes a curtain, with every stitch showing against the outside darkness." The tree trunk is handspun wool, couched to the warp threads. The leaves and figures are all embroidered in white string using combinations of buttonhole

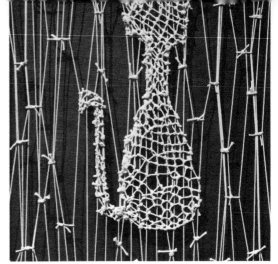

Figure 3-52. Needle-lace cat by another high-school student, Colleen Lynch. Photograph by Jacqueline Enthoven. Both pieces done under instruction of Sister Betty Paquin, Holy Names Academy, Seattle.

Figure 3-53. *Summertime,* hanging in needle lace and couching, on evenly spaced warp threads, stretched on a frame, by Merry Bean. Photograph by McLean Photographers.

stitch, chain stitch, stem stitch, and surface darning.

Evenly spaced groups of warp threads are supported by translucent plexiglass, in *Ra*, a 48-inch garden sculpture by Merry Bean (figs. 3-54 and 3-54a). The warp and the stitches — knotted buttonhole filling, chain stitch, and stemstitch band — are all worked in nylon-fishing line and polyester twine. Small ceramic beads were incorporated during the stitching.

Figure 3-54. *Ra*, garden sculpture in Plexiglas, nylon fishing line, and polyester twine, by Merry Bean. Photograph by McLean Photographers.

Figure 3-54a. Detail of *Ra*, shown from the other side. Photograph by McLean Photographers.

Open areas, in contrast to closely stitched areas, are combined with one another in Dolores Glovna's *Masks* (fig. 3-55). Variations of buttonhole stitch and Cretan open filling are stitched between warp threads supported by a wood frame. A fabric backing, set away from the stitching plane, adds dimension by creating a deep shadow pattern.

The work of enthusiastic craftsmen — and the craftsmen themselves — are a constant source of inspiration to me. As you looked through these pages I hope you, too, have become inspired to try some new approaches to traditional techniques.

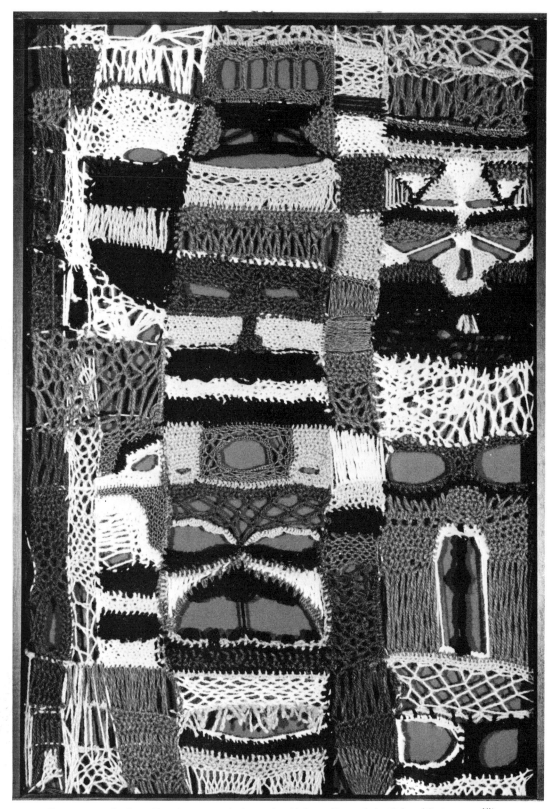

Figure 3-55. *Masks,* framed hanging on stretched warp, in variations of buttonhole stitch and Cretan open filling, by Dolores Glovna. Courtesy of Mrs. Henry J. Soubielle. Photograph by William Eng.

Some Ideas for Finishing

A handsome piece of needlework, labored over and loved, deserves special care in finishing. All too often the craftsman seems to ignore the final step in producing his work, and without that appropriate finishing touch the quality and attention to detail in his work will not be apparent.

Methods of finishing are as varied as your imagination. They need not be costly or elaborate. Sometimes the simplest solutions are the most effective: a hem to hold a rod or a carefully cut cardboard mat.

Many pieces of needle lace and needleweaving have the great advantage of built-in finishing.

They are often suspended in a hoop or frame which becomes a permanent part of the work. Sometimes they are shaped on free-hanging warp threads to be worn as necklaces, collars, or belts. But the great majority of pieces, whatever the techniques, does not end with the stitching. Pressing, stuffing, hemming, binding, mounting, or framing, and hanging will be necessary.

Finishing is a great puzzle to many people, a puzzle that is not difficult to solve if you know where to begin and how to do it. I have tried to answer here the questions most frequently asked by stitchery students.

Pressing and Blocking

Before a piece of embroidery can be framed, mounted,* or stuffed, it must be thoroughly pressed and, in some cases, blocked. As you stitch, try to keep an even but fairly slack tension on the yarn. If you pull too tightly the background fabric will pucker, making the pressing and blocking job a lot harder.

Background fabrics of woven or knit wool, and any wool yarns, are more pliable than cotton, rayon, and linen fabrics or yarns. Stitching too tightly in wool can be corrected by gently pressing the piece into shape with a steam iron. Stitching too tightly in fibers other than wool may often require blocking.

Try pressing without blocking first. Lay a folded terry towel on the ironing board, and then lay the stitchery right-side-down on the towel. Set the iron on steam, and press gently on the wrong side of the work, being careful not to catch the tip of the iron in any long threads. If the stitchery is large, press one section at a time. For more steam, use a damp pressing cloth. Then, spray the whole surface lightly with spray starch and press again with steam or a dry iron. Do not be concerned about flattening the stitches, however textured they may be, as they will sink down into the layers of terry towel. Repeat the steaming and spray starch as necessary.

In working with needle-lace stitches, the blocking technique is very handy, both during and after the stitching. Often it is difficult, on a open warp, to keep the sides of the stitching area from pulling in toward the center. To eliminate this hourglass look, slide a piece of heavy cardboard behind the work, then stick straight pins or T-pins, close together, at right angles through both the work and the cardboard. Spray heavily with spray starch and leave overnight to dry. When you are ready to resume stitching, the mesh will be flat, a little stiff, and straight on the edges.

To block any piece of work, use pre-painted insulation board, available from building suppliers in 4 x 8-foot sheets or 12-inch square tiles. Outline the finished shape on the painted side of the board with a waterproof pen. Lay a layer of clear plastic (a cleaner's bag or a piece cut from a roll) over the drawing. Lay the stitchery right-side-down, over the plastic. Pin through the outline into the board with nonrusting straight pins or T-pins, no more than 1 inch apart. Spray evenly, saturating the surface with clear water from a spray bottle. If you are concerned about either yarn or base fabric colors running, try a test sample first. Leave the blocked piece overnight or until dry, and then remove the piece from the board and press.

Soft Finishing

BACKING THE FINISHED PIECE WITH FABRIC

One of the simplest ways to finish a sampler or hanging is to back it with another piece of fabric. The backing should complement the stitchery in weight, texture, and color. A lightweight cotton needs a lightweight-cotton backing; a heavy wool, a mediumweight-cotton or wool backing. I love men's ties — they always have a surprise inside, a bright, colorful lining to complement the outside pattern. Try a surprise color on the back of your stitchery. Often someone will come up to a finished piece hanging on the wall and automatically pick up a lower corner to look behind. They are delighted with their discovery.

Squaring the Fabric

To prepare the stitchery for backing, the cloth must first be made square. Often stitchers are so anxious to start stitching that they forget to place the work in relation to the weave of the background fabric. It is disappointing to have worked for months on a piece only to discover that it hangs crookedly. To avoid this before stitching, decide on the finished size of your background fabric, adding a 4-inch border all around for finishing. Then, pull out crosswise and lengthwise threads as guides for cutting. The selvage is always parallel with the lengthwise grain of the fabric.

Often a woven material is still crooked even after pulling threads. To remedy this, pull the short diagonal corners away from one another. The long diagonal corners should pull in to make the piece square.

Square a completed piece of embroidery by these same two methods.

Bookbinder's Corner

An easy way to turn in a neat hem around a square or rectangular fabric is to use the bookbinder's corner. Decide on the size of the finished work, then outline the area with contrasting basting stitches. Trim as necessary to make the hem on each edge approximately 1½ inches wide (fig. 4-1, 1). Turn in a corner at right angles, toward the back of the work, with the fold just touching the corner of the basted line (2). Pin

in place, press, and cut off the point to reduce bulkiness. Turn the top edge A and then left-side edge B toward the back on the basting lines (3). Pin and press. Follow the same steps for all four corners. Then tack the mitered folds together on the wrong side with matching sewing thread (4).

To cut a backing, lay the hemmed work on the backing fabric to use as a pattern, then cut out around the edges. Make the same bookbinder's corners on the backing piece, turning the edges in only about 1 inch. Then, with wrong sides together, center the smaller backing, and pin to the larger front (5). Hand stitch with matching sewing thread, taking small stitches first into the folded edge of the backing, then into the hem of the stitchery, and being careful not to go all the way through to the front of the work. For hanging, attach loops to the top edge (see fig. 4-8).

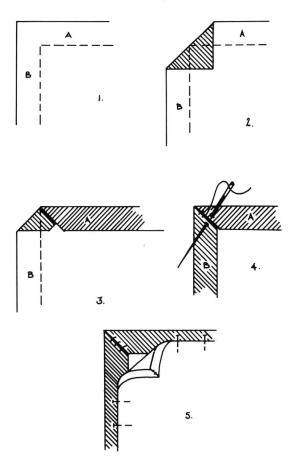

Figure 4-1. Bookbinder's corner for hemming.

Pillowcase Technique

The pillowcase technique (fig. 4-2) allows you to finish the stitchery for hanging with only a few simple steps. Square the fabric, as described earlier, on both the work and the backing. Decide on the size of the finished piece, and then outline this area with contrasting basting stitches. Trim away excess fabric to leave a ⅝-inch seam allowance. Cut the backing exactly the same size, using the front as a pattern. With right sides facing, pin and baste both pieces together. Machine stitch along the seam line starting at the top of the work at A (1), stitching in the direction of the arrows first to B, then from A to C. Stitching each side this way — in the same direction, rather than in a continuous line from B to C — reduces the danger of stretching the material out of shape, which may cause the finished piece to hang crookedly.

Trimming or layering the seam allowance reduces bulkiness in the pillowcase, making it lie flat when it is turned and pressed. Without trimming, the corners will be rounded and the fabric edges will make a ridge in the front of the work. To trim, cut across each corner and layer the seam allowance to make the back ⅜-inch deep and the front ½-inch deep (2) producing a ¼-inch overhang at the front.

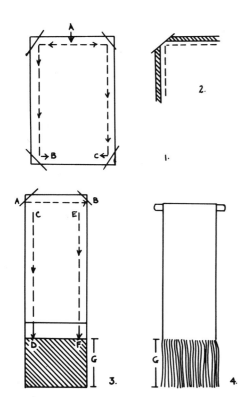

Figure 4-2. The pillowcase technique for backing a finished stitchery with fabric.

Turn the pillowcase right side out, and press thoroughly. Close the opening between B and C (1) by hand stitching the folded edges together along the basted line. Attach loops for hanging (see fig. 4-8).

A variation of the pillowcase technique (3), can be made by first hemming the lower edge of the backing so it is 4 to 6 inches shorter than the stitchery. Machine stitch across the top seam allowance from A to B. Trim off the corners. Stitch from C, which should be 1½ inches below A B, over the hem to D, and then from E to F. Turn the work right side out, and press thoroughly. Pull out the crosswise filling threads in the lower area G (4), leaving the lengthwise threads to make a decorative fringe. Finally, slide a rod for hanging through the top, between the fabric layers.

STUFFING

Materials

Stuffing inside a fabric envelope or a shaped construction can add dimensional form far beyond the simple pillow and cube shapes described below, but it follows the same basic principles. Materials for stuffing, whether hidden or a visual part of the finished work, can be of the most fanciful materials or simply stuffing purchased at your local variety store.

Styrofoam (plastic foam) blocks can be cut with a bread knife or fine saw to fit inside any shape. Nylon stockings, washed, cut up, and packed in firmly, make a smooth finished outside surface. Foam-rubber chips are messy to work with but ideal for a pillow — they pack down slightly but plump up easily again. Lightweight and flying Styrofoam pellets are also messy to handle and make a gravel-like surface inside all but very heavy fabrics. For quilts, cloudlike polyester batting from the Sears Roebuck catalog comes in rolls, and can be cut in any shape without pulling apart.

Use a rope for stuffing in a tubular construction by covering it with cloth or yarn. Make a pocket of needle lace to fill with unspun wool or gathered treasures (fig. 4-3).

Stuffing a Pillow

Pillows of all shapes and sizes can add brightness and comfort to almost any room. Because of the wear and tear they get — they are leaned on, sat on, thrown, and held — they need an easily removable cover that can be dry cleaned. One of the bright moments in my life was discovering how easy it is to put a zipper in a pillow cover. For years I puzzled over how to sew up three sides,

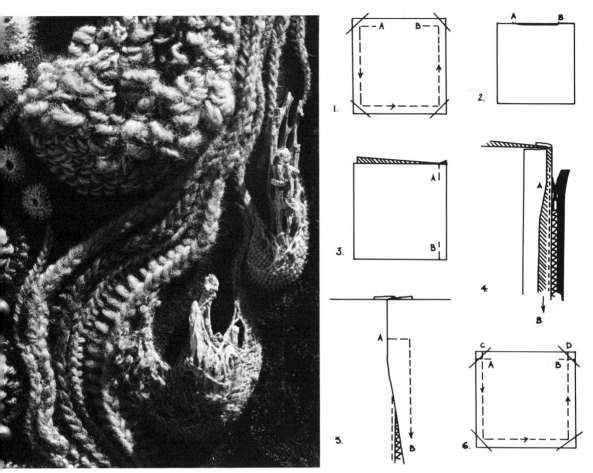

Figure 4-3. Detail of *Anywhere That's Wild* (fig. 3-4), by Wilcke Smith, showing a unique approach to stuffing.

Figure 4-4. Making a pillow.

then put a zipper in the fourth. Impossible? Read on.

Stitchery, needlepoint, appliqué, and quilting all work well for pillows. To make the finished piece into a square or rectangular shape (fig. 4-4), first outline the seam line with contrasting basting thread. Cut away the excess fabric, leaving a ½- to ⅝-inch seam allowance. Choose a backing fabric to complement the front, and cut it to the same size.

Next, cut two equal pieces of unbleached muslin or cotton broadcloth, the same size as the front and back, to hold the stuffing. Seam the muslin by machine stitching from A around three sides to B (1). Trim off the corners, turn the seams to the inside, and stuff firmly with foam-rubber chips. Pin and hand stitch the opening between A and B with matching sewing thread (2).

Now for the cover. Measure the length of the metal part of your zipper. It should be approximately 4 inches shorter than the full length of the side it will be set into. Center that dimension on the seam allowance, marking the ends of the metal part at points A and B (3). Pin. Machine stitch the 2-inch seam from the top edge to A, then the 2-inch seam from B to the lower edge. Press the seam open, including the opening between A and B.

Fold back the seam allowance on the left side ⅛ to ¼ inch, and baste to the cloth on the left side of the zipper. Using a zipper foot, machine stitch the same line close to the folded edge (4). With the right side out and the seam opened flat, top stitch from A to B (5), being sure to catch in the cloth on the right side of the zipper.

Before stitching the three remaining sides of the pillow, be sure to open the zipper. Pin the right sides together, machine stitch from C around to D (6), trim off the corners, and turn right side out, through the open zipper. Press carefully, put the stuffed muslin pillow inside, and close the zipper.

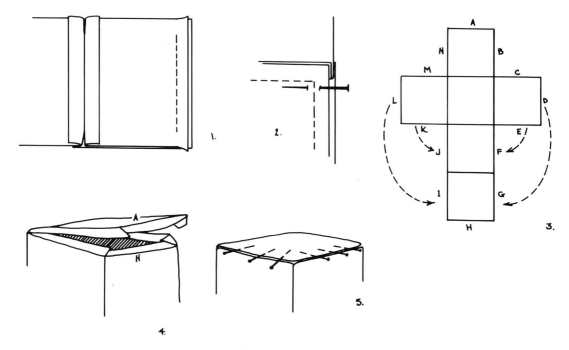

Figure 4-5. Making a cube-shaped soft sculpture.

Stuffing a Cube

For a decorative, cube-shaped, soft sculpture, you will need six square pieces of the background fabric. If the cloth or canvas does not ravel, the pieces may be cut out first, allowing a ½- to ⅝-inch seam allowance. If the cloth is lightweight and ravels easily, outline each square with a basting thread or colored pencil. Stretch the piece intact on a hoop or frame to do the embroidery, then cut the finished squares apart.

Work a design on each piece. The sides may be quite similar, each worked in the same color range, but using a great variety of stitches. When assembled, the cube must be held and turned, in order to view all sides. Try introducing an element of surprise by stitching each square in a completely different color and texture. Perhaps the background fabric itself could be varied by using contrasting solid colors, a pattern or a stripe.

When the embroidery on all six squares is complete, join four squares to make a strip. With right sides together, machine stitch between the seam allowances only (fig. 4-5, 1). Next, pin and stitch the two remaining pieces (2) to the sides of the second square to make a T-shape (3). Press all the seams open, and trim away the corners of the seam allowance to reduce bulk.

Now, with right sides together, seam the edges E to F and K to J, then D to G and L to I (3). Press

these seams open using a sleeve board or fabric-covered stick to reach inside the box. Trim away extra fabric at the corners, where the seams meet.

Turn the cube inside out. Press the seam allowance to the inside around the top edge of the box and around the lid (4).

For stuffing, measure the inside finished dimensions of the cube, then cut a Styrofoam (plastic foam) block to fit the space exactly. If you prefer to use cut-up nylon stockings or shredded foam rubber, make the opening in the cube smaller by joining the edges N to M before turning.

Pin the lid shut (5), and then seam the remaining sides by hand with a sharp needle and sewing thread, taking small stitches alternately into one folded edge then the other.

BINDING THE EDGES WITH FABRIC

Author Jean Ray Laury devised a method of binding the edges of a cut-through appliqué with narrow strips of fabric in a matching or contrasting color. You can borrow this binding technique (fig. 4-6) not only for the layered cut through, but also for any single layer stitchery or perhaps a quilt. You can choose any width for the binding. It can be very narrow, like piping, or very wide, which makes a small background fabric look larger.

148

First, square the fabric. Then, cut four strips for the binding (1). Two should be the same length as the background, for sides C and D, and the other two should be 2 inches longer than the width of the background, for sides A and B. A good rule to determine the width of the strips is to cut the piece four times as wide as you want the finished binding; i.e., if the binding is to be 1 inch wide, the strip should be 4 inches wide.

Seam the first two side pieces C and D to the work. Line up the edges, right sides together (1), and then determine the seam line by measuring in from the edge to the width of the finished binding. Machine stitch from edge A to edge B on this line. If the stitchery on the background has been worked too close to the edge, and the binding is being used as a visual extension of the work, this first seam may be as small as ¼ inch.

Press the seam flat on the right side of the work, with the seam allowance towards C (2). Press the strip to the back, using the seam allowance as a guide for the fold (3). Turn the work over, then press the outside edge of the strip in, to meet the edge of the seam allowance (4). Fold the outside edge in, and pin it to the back of the work. Hand stitch, first into the fold, then into the fabric, using tiny stitches to avoid going through to the front of the work (5). Attach a similar binding to edge D (6) by following steps shown in Diagrams 2 through 5.

When the sides C and D are complete, seam one of the longer strips to edge A (7). Press as before (2) and turn the work over (8). Now, fold in the 1-inch extension on both ends and press, (9). Follow steps shown in Diagrams 4 and 5 to finish the top (10), then repeat for edge B.

To hang the bound piece, you can leave the hem open on the back of edge A, tacking only the ends together. Slide a flat stick, the full width of the piece, between the binding and the back of the work. Attach a sawtooth picture hanger in the back by tacking through the binding and into the wood.

FRINGING

Fringing is an excellent way to add length and texture to a finished stitchery. If you find the background fabric is too long for the embroidery, pull out the filling threads in the excess to leave the warp as a loose fringe (see fig. 4-2), rather than cutting the piece off. These threads can be knotted, wrapped, stitched with various bar stitches, or left plain.

If the background fabric is too short, add length with a yarn fringe, or work one of the many stitched edgings to combine with a fringe.

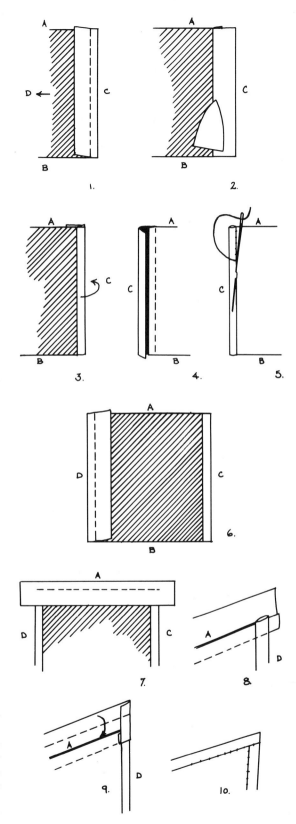

Figure 4-6. Binding the edges of a finished stitchery with fabric strips. This technique is also useful in cut-through appliqué.

149

Figure 4-7. Wrapped fringe in detail from *Feuervogel* (fig. 3-46), by Barbara Meier.

WAYS OF HANGING

Loops

After the stitchery is bound or backed, attach loops at the top edge for hanging. Loops can be skinny or fat, and made of fabric or yarn or any other suitable material. Fabric and yarn must be cut and sewn; felt, plastic, and leather can be attached directly after cutting, as there is no problem with raw edges. Their size and spacing should be in proportion to the stitchery. A small lightweight piece needs narrow, widely spaced loops; a large, heavy piece needs wide or closely spaced loops to support its weight.

To cut the fabric, decide on the width of the finished loop, double it, and add ½ to ⅝ inch to each edge for a seam allowance. The length of the strip will be double the finished height plus 2½ inches for attaching in the back. Often loops are made out of scraps of background fabric, but if you have enough fabric to make the loops from one long piece and cut them apart later, it is faster. Seam the whole strip, then cut equal pieces for the individual loops.

With the right sides of the fabric together, line up the cut edges, and machine stitch lengthwise along the seam allowance from A to B (fig. 4-8,1). Press the seam open, and then turn the tube so the seam is on the inside. Press again, with the seam down the middle of one side (2). If the loop is narrow, fasten a large safety pin through a

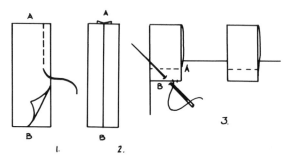

Figure 4-8. Making fabric loops for hanging a stitchery from a rod.

single layer of fabric at one end of the tube. Thread the pin down through the inside and out through the other end, working the bunched cloth along with your fingers as you go.

Turn in a ½-inch hem on edge B, and press. Space the loops evenly along the top of the stitchery, and pin them to the back of the work. With hand stitching, first attach edge A, 1 inch below the top of the stitchery, then fold down edge B and attach 1 inch below A (3). This layering of the edges makes a smooth joining that will not show through on the front of the work.

Make yarn loops by wrapping the thread several times through the stitchery and around a rod (fig. 4-9, 1). On the third round, bind the threads together snugly against the rod with a knotted stitch (2). Work overcasting stitches tightly down around the vertical threads toward the top of the stitchery (3). To end the thread, loosen the overcasting slightly with the tip of the needle, then thread it up through the core and out between two stitches (4). Snip off the end of the thread.

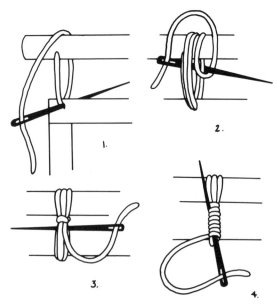

Figure 4-9. Making yarn loops for hanging.

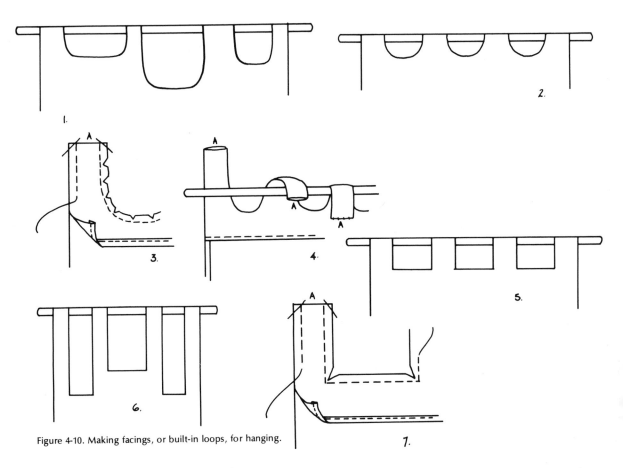

Figure 4-10. Making facings, or built-in loops, for hanging.

Facings

Facing is a way of making built-in loops at the top of a finished stitchery (fig. 4-10). Before starting the stitching, plan to allow an extra width of matching fabric to use for the facing.

The design of the cut-out areas can be curved or squared, in regular or irregular patterns (1, 2, 5, and 6). Consider the compatibility of the design of the facing with the design of the stitchery. Finish a definitely circular motif with a curved facing or a geometrical, squared pattern with a squared facing.

First, determine the position and the thickness of the rod, and how far below the rod the cut-out areas will extend. Draw and cut a paper pattern to include the seam allowances, extending the top of the loops 3 to 4 inches above the rod line.

Press and machine stitch a narrow hem in the lower edge of the facing (3). Lay the facing on the stitchery, right sides together, then machine stitch down the side seams and around the seam allowances (3). Trim off the corners at the open end A, and cut out notches around the curve to reduce bulkiness and make the fabric lie flat. Turn right-side-out and press. Turn in the raw edge at A and press. Fold all the loops over the

rod toward the back, adjust, and pin in place. Hand stitch along A, through the facing only (4). For a squared cut-out shape, stitch and trim away excess fabric as shown (7).

Finish the bottom corners with the bookbinder's corner, then back with fabric, as demonstrated in Figure 4-1. Or, sew another facing to the bottom to hold a second rod.

Rod Pockets

Any horizontal rigid object used to support a fabric hanging must be threaded through loops or a loose hem in the cloth. Choose the size of the rod you will be using before starting to stitch. Before cutting the background fabric, determine extra length needed for the rod pocket by wrapping the fabric loosely around the rod and adding 2 inches more.

Back the finished stitchery with fabric, using the pillowcase technique (see fig. 4-2). Make the backing 1 inch shorter than the front. Then make the opening at the top edge A (fig. 4-11, 1). Fold down edge A over the backing and machine stitch close to the raw edge through all layers (2). Wrap A loosely over the rod (3) and pin to the backing,

151

adjusting the hem to allow the rod to slide in and out easily. With the rod out, hand stitch edge A to the backing, taking care not to stitch through to the front of the work.

For an open, lacy stitchery to be viewed from either side, perhaps as a screen, eliminate the backing (4). Sew a narrow hem in all four sides, sew rod pockets at both ends, and hang.

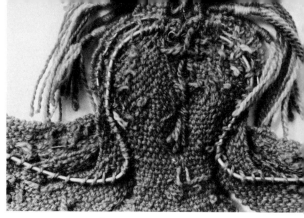

Figure 4-12. Detail of *Feuervogel* (fig. 3-46) by Barbara Meier, showing wire threaded through the back of the work, to support and hang the finished piece.

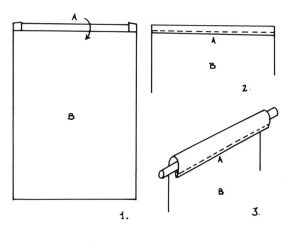

Figure 4-11. Making a rod pocket.

Figure 4-13. Weaving, by Carole Sabiston, hung from a curved piece of driftwood that echoes the circular design.

Rods

Rods for hanging can be of many designs, ornate or plain, and in metal, plexiglass, or wood. Use any rigid object as long as it is strong enough to support the stitchery.

Cut solid ⅜-inch brass curtain rods to any length with a hacksaw. Haunt antique shops for gnarled wrought iron or sections of brass headboards. Attach a decorative finial or drawer knob to the ends of a wood or brass rod. Find a builder or lumber yard supplying wood dowels. They range from ¼-inch diameter, to the 1¼-inch closet-pole size. If you live near or travel to a beach, look for pieces of driftwood for hanging.

Let the support for your stitchery be individual and exciting, always a complement to the work itself, rather than a distraction.

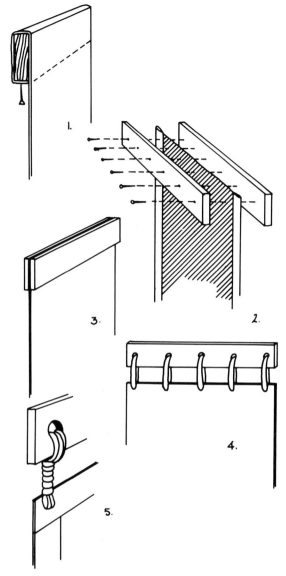

Figure 4-14. Ways of using wood strips for hanging.

Make a sandwich of two thin boards with the finished stitchery between (2). Bind the stitchery on three edges, leaving a raw edge at the top. Cut, sand, and finish the two identical boards, then drill holes for screws through the back board. Assemble (2) with the top of the fabric slightly below the top of the boards. The screws must not be any longer than the thickness of one board plus half the thickness of the other, or they will go through to the front. Attach picture hangers to the back and hang (3).

Try drilling holes in a board to thread leather thongs (4), or yarn loops through (5).

Wood Finishing

I often use acrylic paint as a wood finish. It is available in tubes from art-supply stores. Almost any color can be mixed if you keep on hand the clear primary colors, red, yellow, and blue, along with an umber, a black, and a white. The colors are water soluble, can be mixed in small quantities in a Styrofoam meat tray, can be brushed on easily, and dry within an hour. Applied with a cloth, watered down acrylics look like stain.

If you prefer a real stain, keep a small tin of dark oak wood stain on hand. For variety, mix with a little olive green oil paint from a tube. Be prepared to wait at least overnight for an oil-base stain to dry.

To finish woods such as teak and oak, buy a jar of mineral oil from the pharmacy, and rub it into the wood with a soft cloth.

Hard Finishing

Matting

Cutting a cardboard mat is really not difficult if you have the right tool. A good mat knife with spare sharp blades stored inside a sturdy handle can be purchased at any art supply or stationery store. Some people like to use a metal straight-edge as a guide for cutting but if it slips ever so slightly the mat is ruined.

I have a favorite method for cutting that perhaps you will like, too. Draw a pencil line around the area to be cut out. With the mat knife, start at one corner and pull carefully toward you along the line, pressing lightly, to make a shallow cut in the board. Continue all the way around the outline. This shallow cut acts as a guide for the knife. On the second round, press down hard and the knife will stay in the groove. Make sharp corners with the sharp point of the blade. After the second round the cut part should fall free from the mat.

Wood Strips

Wood strips or boards are easy to cut, to finish, and to assemble (fig. 4-14). The tools — a saw, screws, nails, a screwdriver, a hammer, and some sandpaper — can be found in almost any home. Often a local building materials supplier or lumberyard is willing to cut small pieces of wood to order.

Hem or bind the sides and lower edge of a finished stitchery, wrap the top around a smooth but unfinished 1 x 2-inch wood strip, and tack the cloth to the under side (1). Attach some flat sawtooth picture hangers to the back of the wood through the fabric. The panel will hang away from the wall, making a deep shadow that gives it added dimension.

Mat board, in 18 x 20-inch or 20 x 30-inch sheets, is stocked in art supply stores and comes in a wide range of colors. Poster board, in 22 x 28-inch sheets, is widely stocked at art counters in discount stores. This is a thinner cardboard, finished on both sides with glossy brilliant colors.

Window mats can be any shape — square, rectangular, oval, circular. To cut a circular window, mark the outline first with a compass or draw around a plate, bowl or pot lid. Cut out the circle with a mat knife as directed above. Cut once around first, turning the cardboard as you go, to make a groove for the knife. Press hard and through to the back on the second round. When the cut-out section falls free from the mat, file the cut edges smooth with an emery board.

A good way to mount a piece of fabric is to make a cardboard sandwich (fig. 4-15). You will need two pieces of mat board exactly the same size, one for the window mat and one for the backing. Measure and cut the window, leaving at least a 2-inch border on all four sides. For a more rectangular look, leave a wider border at the bottom, as traditionally done in fine-art matting.

Lay the two pieces with right sides down and the two top ends together on a flat surface. Make a hinge by taping along the seam with 1½-inch masking tape (1). Adjust the stitchery (A) on the inside so it appears in the correct position in the window, then tape it to the backing on all four edges (2). Close the sandwich, and the mat is finished. A round sandwich mat works especially well when the stitchery is slightly padded, making it stick out a little through the cut circle.

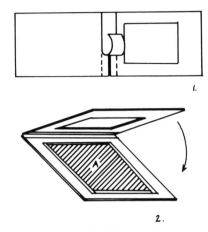

Figure 4-15. Mounting a fabric in a cardboard sandwich mat.

Stretching and Double Mounting

Stretching fabric on a frame or oil canvas stretcher is described on page 13. Follow the same method for mounting a finished stitchery on a piece of the ⅜-inch plywood. Do not use ¼-inch plywood, as it tends to warp, or ½-inch plywood, which is too heavy. A commercial product, not too readily available to the general

Figure 4-16. Child's stitchery, by Christopher Nordfors at age 3, is mounted in a circular cardboard sandwich mat. Padding behind the stitchery makes a rounded surface.

public but ideal for mounting stitchery, is a light-weight board made of a Styrofoam core between two layers of cardboard.

Double mounting is a frameless finishing technique employing the layering of two separate boards. The large one is stretched with plain fabric and placed behind a smaller one stretched with stitchery (fig. 4-17). The fabric on the back board should complement the stitchery in texture and in color, taking the place of a frame by making a decorative border around the work. Join the two pieces with no less than four screws from the back. The screws should be no longer than the total thickness of one board plus one half the thickness of the other, as they can create an unwanted additional texture if they stick through the delicate embroidery.

Another version of double mounting adds great depth and an exciting shadow pattern to an open, lacy stitchery. If the finished piece has been worked on a wooden frame or a heavy cardboard mat (see fig. 1-33), cover a piece of plywood that is the same size as the mat with a solid-color, contrasting fabric. Mount the stitchery away from the backing, using wood strips as spacers if necessary. Then bind the two edges together with a simple wood frame.

White or off-white needle-made laces, antique or contemporary, can be attractively appliquéd to a bright solid-color fabric, and then double mounted as before.

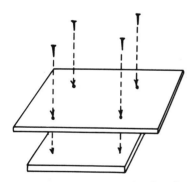

Figure 4-17. Making a double mounting for a frameless hanging.

Framing

Mention of the word framing conjures up visions either of expensive custom framing or of struggling yourself with unruly little pieces of wood, nails, and glue. Making your own frames need not be difficult if you have the right tools. The purchase of a miter box and a set of corner clamps makes the job a lot more fun. The miter box is a fine saw, mounted on a horizontal surface, with clamps to hold the wood. The saw can

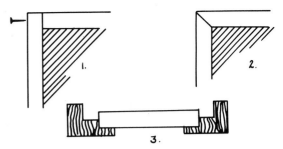

Figure 4-18. Framing: (1) butt joint, (2) mitered joint, (3) custom molding.

be easily adjusted to cut 45- and 90-degree angles, and so is equally handy for making straight cuts and the 45-degree angles that mitering corners requires. A corner clamp holds two sides of a cut molding together at right angles while the glue dries in the mitered joint.

Any molding, simple or ornate, can be made into a frame by mitering the corners. Some custom framing shops will sell their pre-finished molding by the foot. Or, check the local builder's supplier for baseboard and ceiling trims used by carpenters. A molding with an extra lip inside (fig. 4-18, 3) is one of my favorites for stitchery. It gives the work a little breathing space while setting it off with a dark shadow.

Perhaps you will only want to make a frame occasionally. Then flat wood strips and a minimum of tools are needed. With a small metal square, mark the wood for a straight cut, saw, then fasten the corners together with ¾-inch brads, using a butt joint (fig. 4-18, 1). Fit the finished frame around a stitchery stretched on ⅜-inch plywood. Fasten it in place with more brads, nailed from the outside through the frame and into the plywood.

Metal section frames, sold in art supply and frame shops, come in aluminum or brass finish and in many lengths to the inch. They are easily and quickly assembled. The inside groove to hold the work is narrow, so stretch the stitchery on ¼-inch plywood or heavy cardboard. The rigid frame will keep the work from warping.

Stock frames should not be overlooked. They come in a great variety of colors and styles. Their only drawback is a loss of freedom in your creativity, if the size and shape of your work is determined before you begin.

One last step in the finishing process is to spray the work heavily with Scotchgard or a similar fabric protector. Any dust the fabric or textured areas may collect then can be brushed off easily rather than penetrating the fibers. If you are concerned about the use of these spray products on particular fabrics or yarns, check the label on the can or make a test on an extra swatch.

Bibliography

Anchor Manual of Needlework. Boston: Charles T. Branford Co., 3rd ed.,1968.

Caplin, Jessie F., *The Lace Book*. New York: Macmillan, 1932.

Caulfield, S.F.A. and Saward, Blanche C. *Encyclopedia of Victorian Needlework* (Dictionary of Needlework). Vols. I - II. New York: Dover Publications Inc.,1972.

Christie, Mrs. Archibald. *Samplers and Stitches*. Great Neck, New York: American Publication, Hearthside Press Inc., 1971.

DeDillmont, Th. *Encyclopedia of Needlework*. Alsace, France: Mulhouse, n.d.

Emery, Irene. *The Primary Structures of Fabrics*.Washingon D.C.: The Textile Museum. (New York: The Spiral Press).1966.

Enthoven, Jacqueline. *The Stitches of Creative Embroidery*. New York: Van Nostrand Reinhold, 1964.

Harvey, Virginia. "Looping—I," *Threads in Action,* Vol. 4, No. 2, Winter 1972–3.

—————————"Looping—II," *Threads in Action*, Vol. 4, No. 3, Spring 1973.

—————————"Patterned Netting," *Threads in Action*, Vol. 4, No. 1, Fall 1972.

Karasz, Mariska. *Adventures in Stitches*. New York: Funk and Wagnalls, 1959.

Petersen, Grete and Svennas, Elsie. *Handbook of Stitches*. New York: Van Nostrand Reinhold, 1959.

Powys, Marian. *Lace and Lace Making*. Boston: Charles, T. Branford Co., 1953.

Thomas, Mary. *Dictionary of Embroidery Stitches*. New York: William Morrow and Co., 1935.

Index of Stitches

Italic numbers indicate photographs.

A

 Antwerp edging stitch   59, *61*

 Armenian edging stitch   61

B

 backstitch   15

 band in interlacing   91, *92*

 braid-edging stitch   60

 buttonhole attachments   28, 29

 buttonholed bars   *20,* 101, 102, *103,* 111

 buttonholed half-bar insertion   64, 67

 buttonhole insertion   65, *67*

C

 Ceylon stitch   49, *50*

 chain stitch   15, *11*

 chained bar   104, 106

 chevron stemstitch   71, *73*

 checkered chain band   90, *91*

 coral knots   23

 corded, or overcast, bar   99, 100

 couching   16

 couching with buttonhole stitch   40

 Cretan open filling   76, *77*

 Cretan-stitch insertion   67, 68, *70*

D

 detached buttonhole filling   37

 detached chained bar   104, *105,* 106

157

detached up-and-down buttonhole
filling   50, *51;* variation, 102

 hollie stitch   55

 diamond filling   56, *57*

 honeycomb filling   83, 84, *85*

 double bars with woven-circle filling
88

I

 double buttonhole filling   43, 44;
variation, 110

 interlacing stitch on a base of double
herringbone   *26,* 94, *95*

 double buttonhole filling with
straight-stitch return   *17,* 46

 interlacing stitch on double-herringbone
variation   95, *96*

F

 faggoting   66, *67*

 Italian-buttonhole insertion   62, *63*

 filet stitch   57, *58*

K

G

 knotted buttonhole filling   *14,* 41, 42

 ghost-stitch filling   80, *81*

 knotted double buttonhole filling   47, *48*

H

knotted insertion   66, *67*

 herringbone base for interlacing
93, *94*

knotted grid for filling stitches   80

L

 laced herringbone stitch   93, *94*

 laced insertion   69, 70

 laced lattice filling   87

 lacy buttonhole filling   *12,* 38, 39, *131*

M

 Maltese-cross filling   97, *98*

 Maltese cross in interlacing   98, 99

O

 open buttonhole filling   *12,* 38, 39, *131*

 over-and-under weaving   81, *82,* 98

 overcast bar   99, 100

P

 plaited-edging stitch   61, 62

 plaited insertion   68, 69, *70*

 Portuguese border   90, *91*

R

 raised chain band   *20,* 89

 raised honeycomb filling   79, *80*

 raised-stem spiderweb stitch   72, 74, *75,* 112

 Russian-overcast filling   78

S

 Shi sha glass attachment   26

 single buttonhole filling   *11, 12,* 38, 39

 spaced buttonhole filling   *36,* 43, 44, 46; variation, 110